SHAPES & THINGS

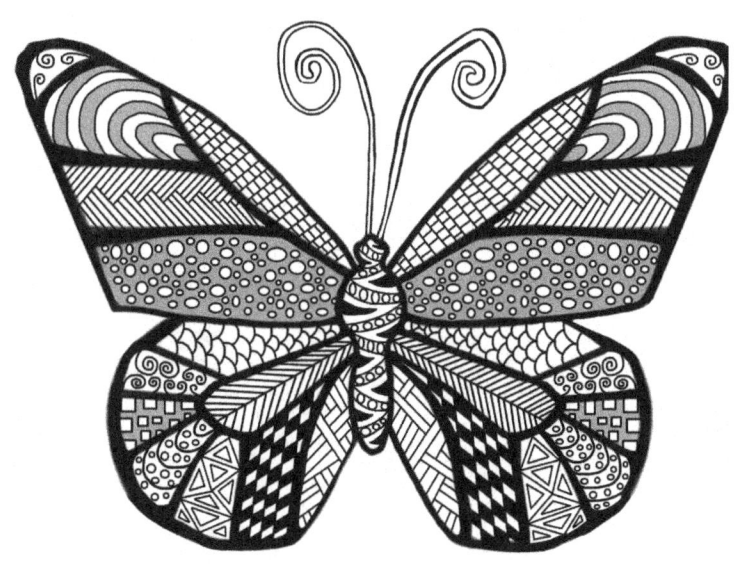

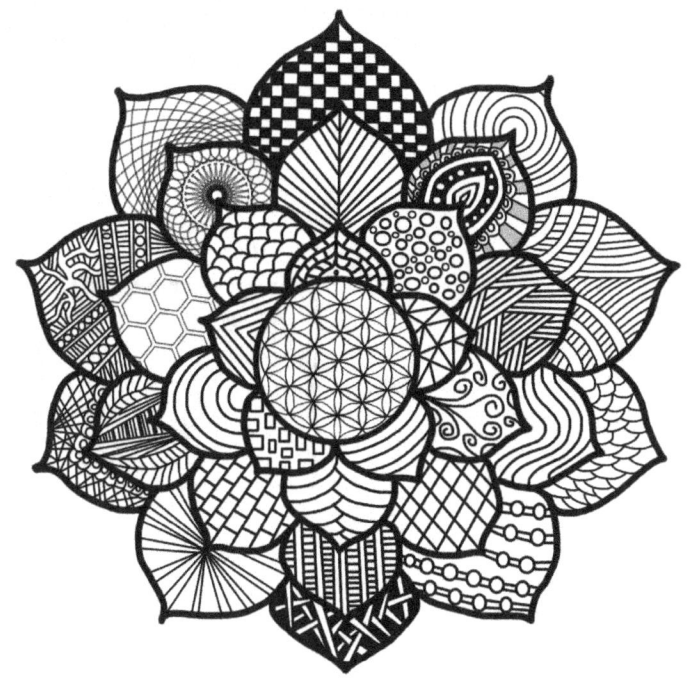

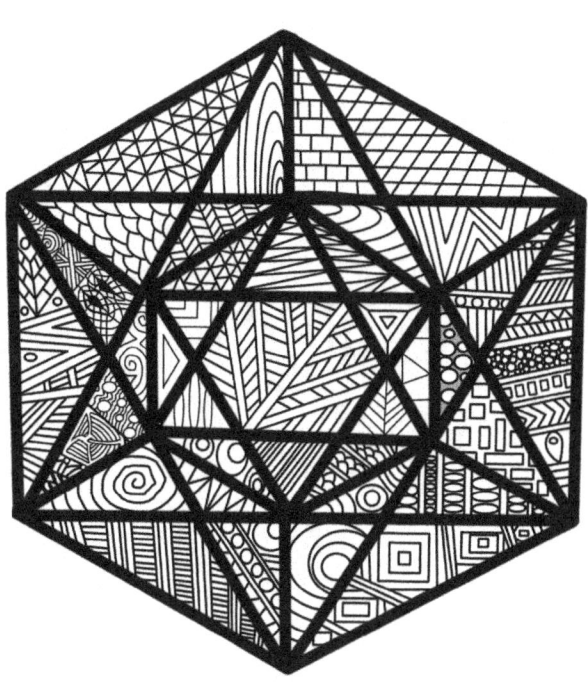

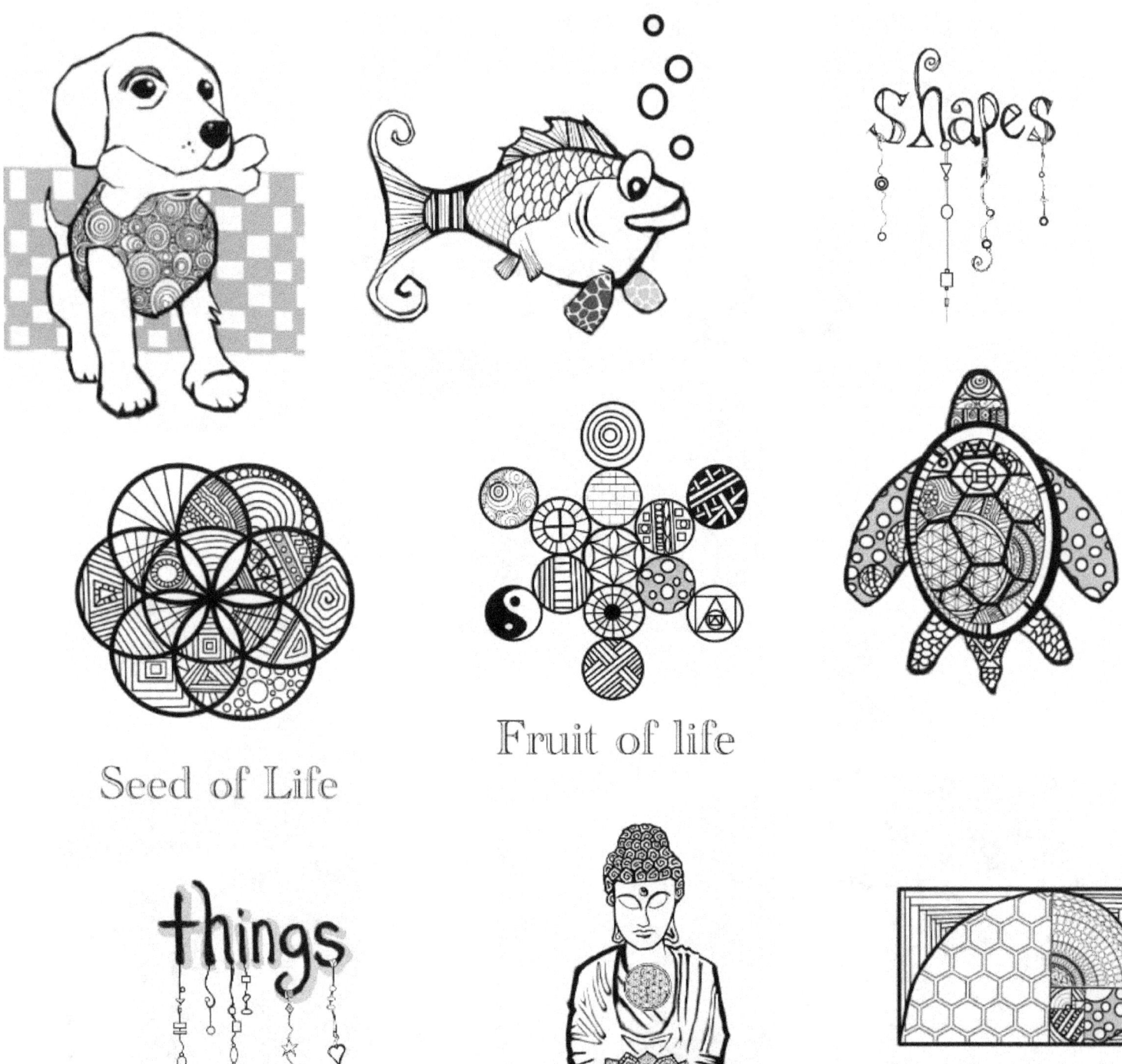

Seed of Life

Fruit of life

shapes

things

Fibonacci

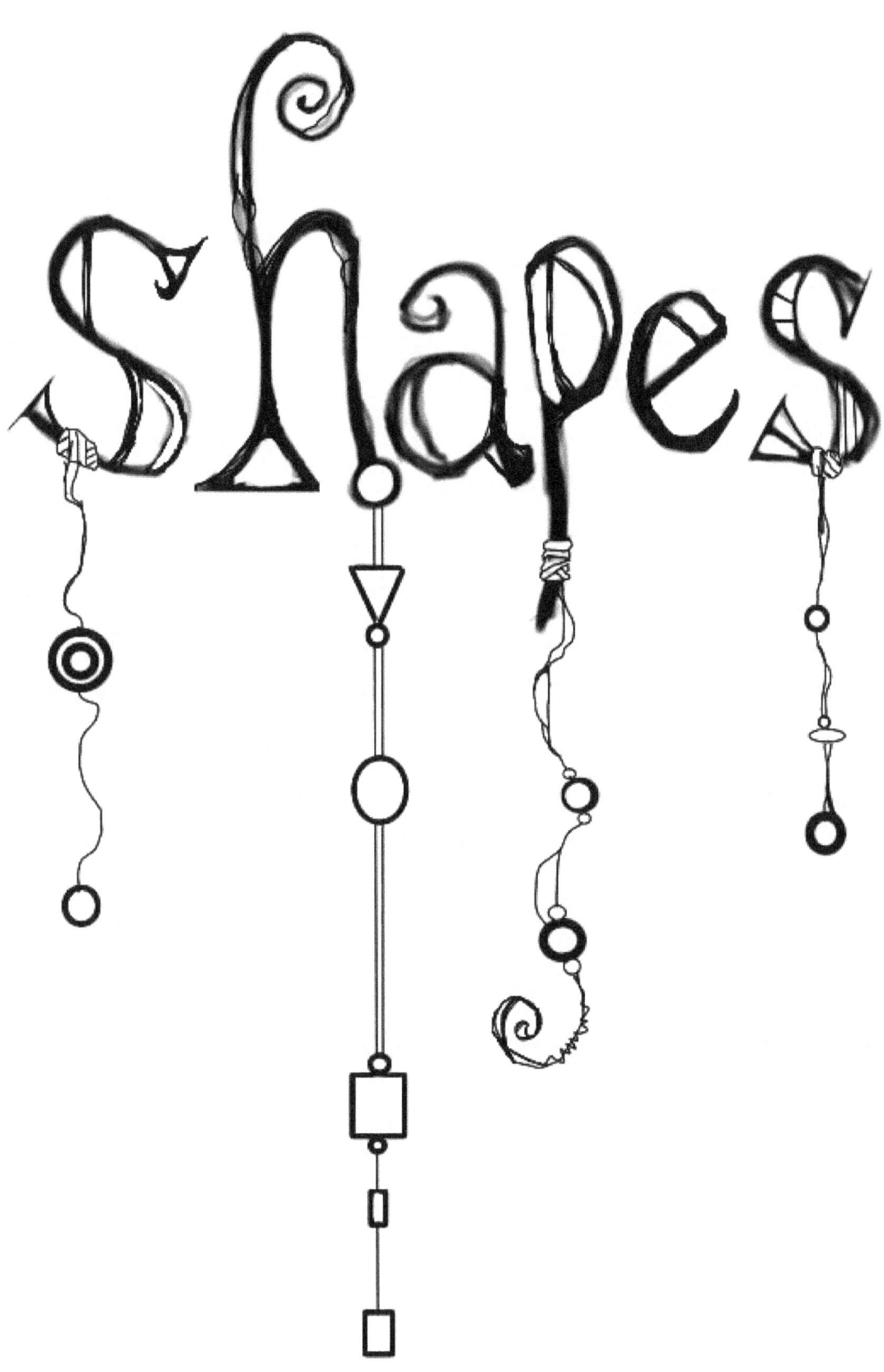

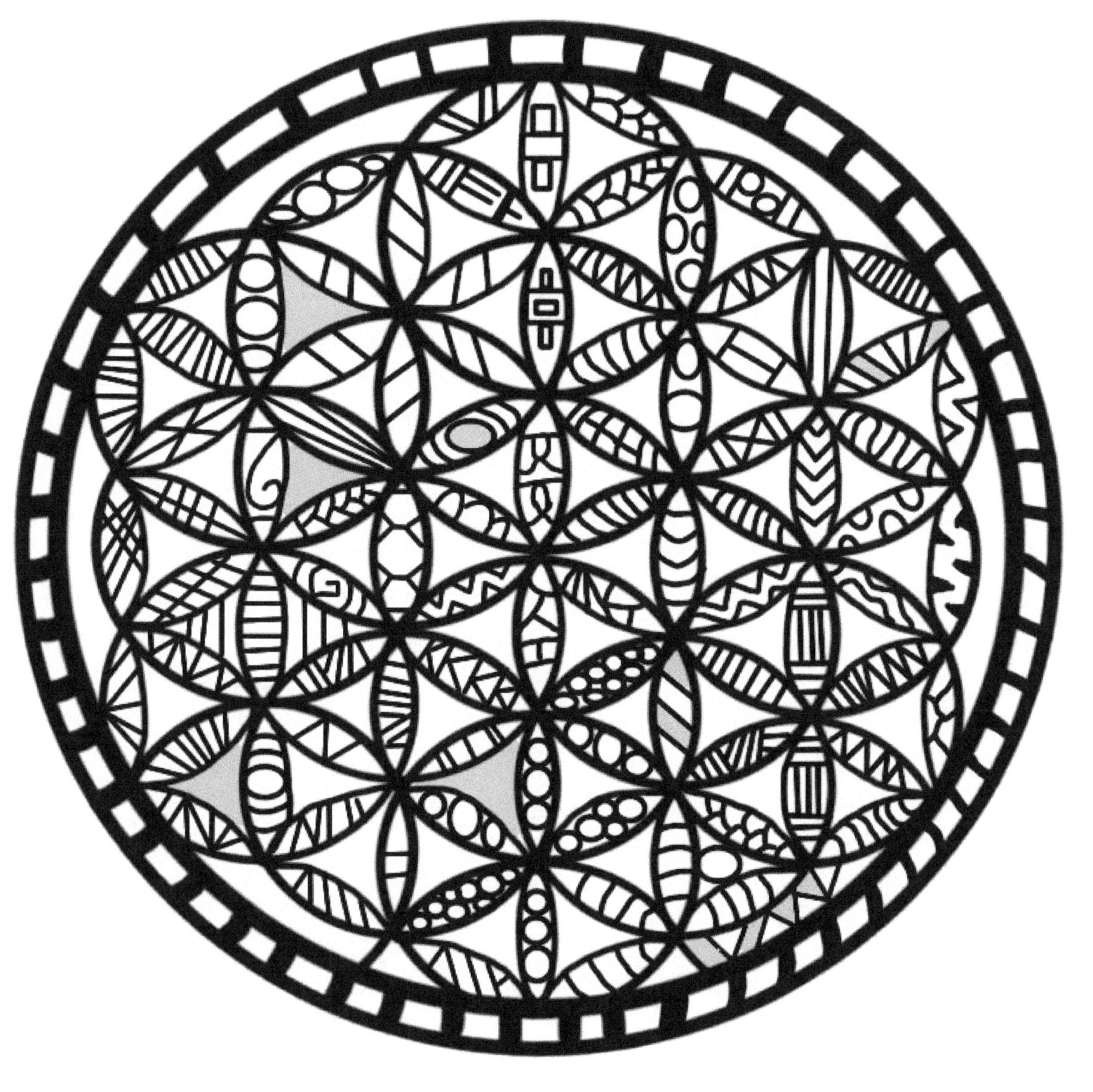

Flower of Life

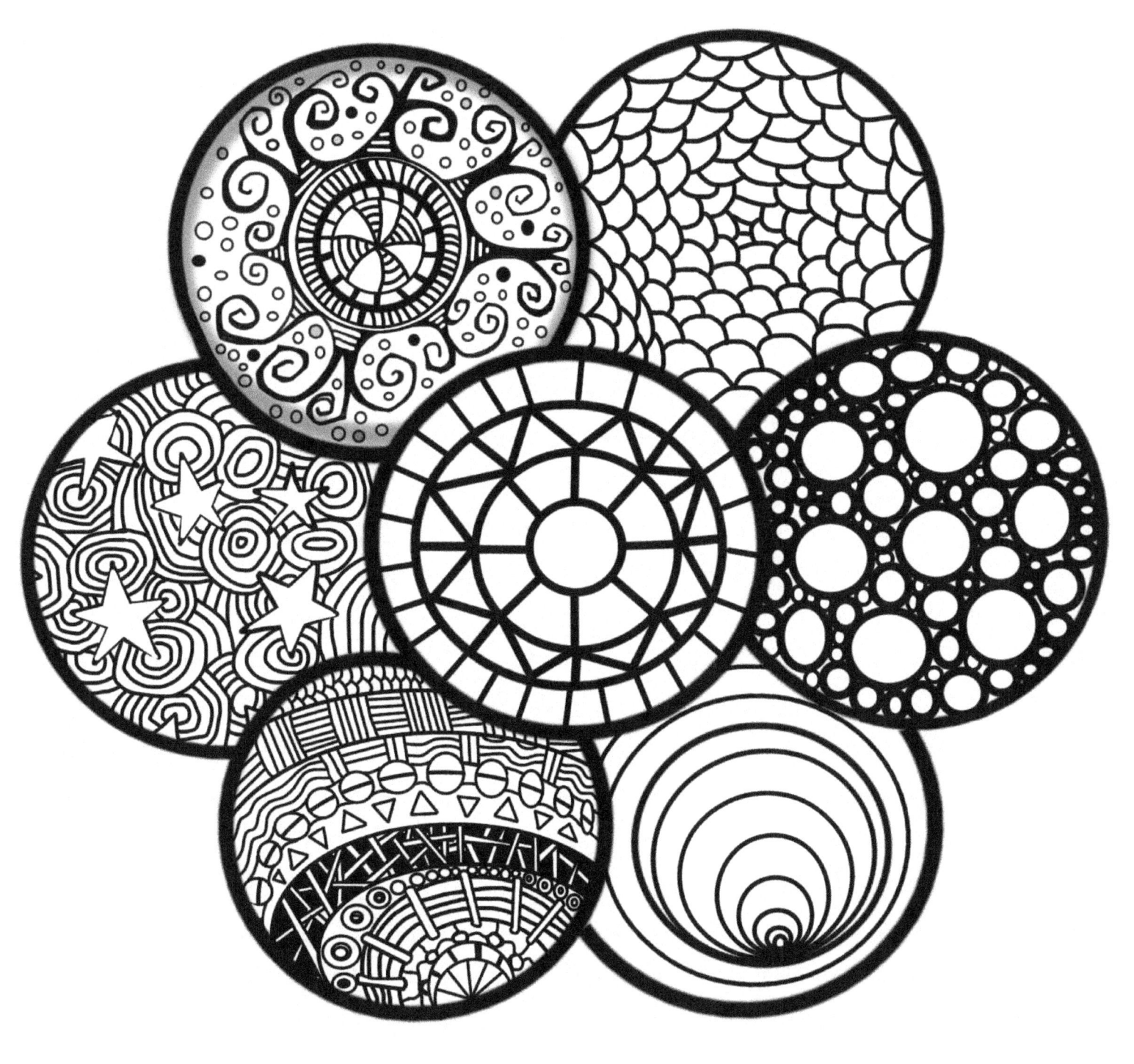

Egg of Life

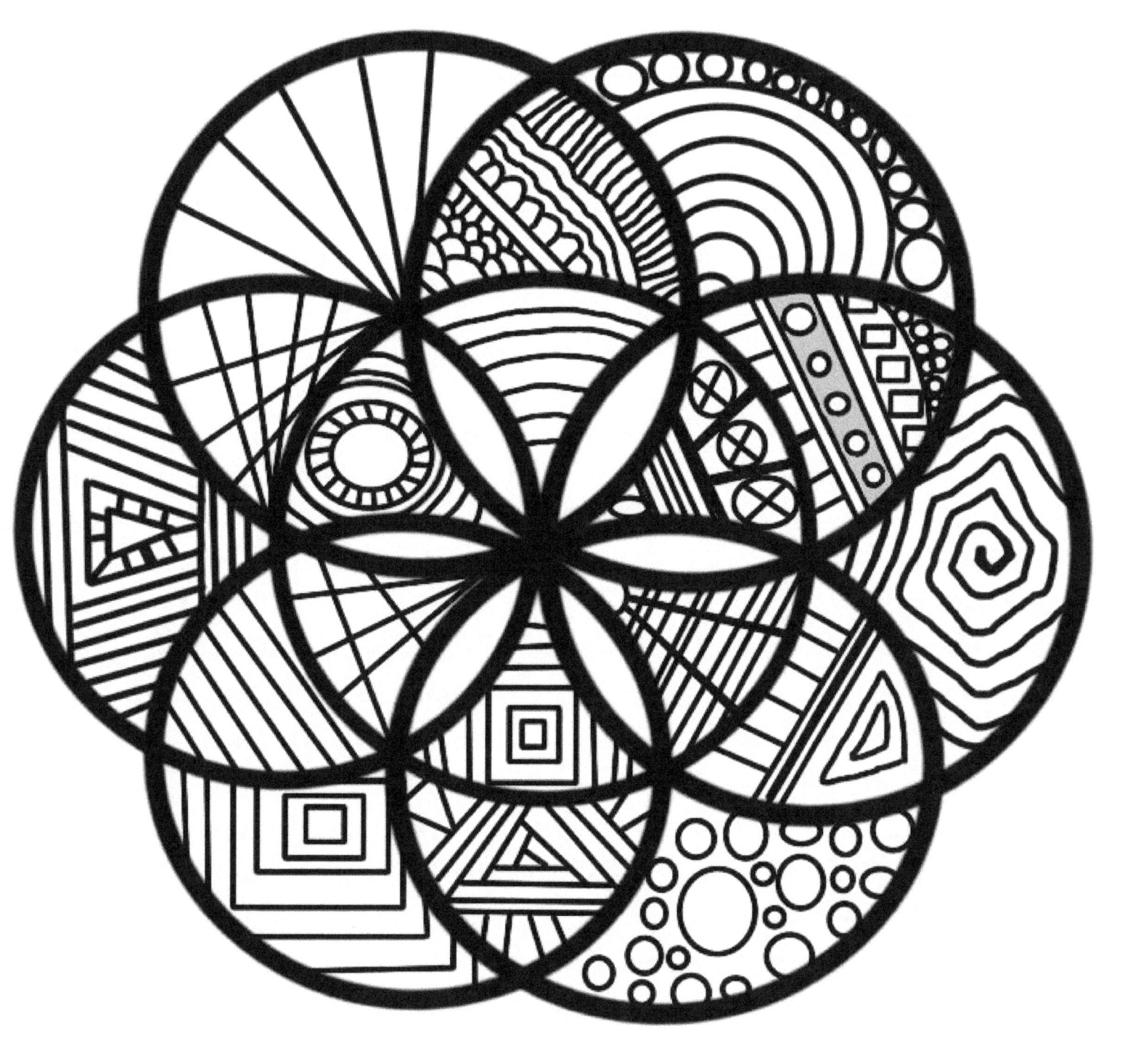

Seed of Life

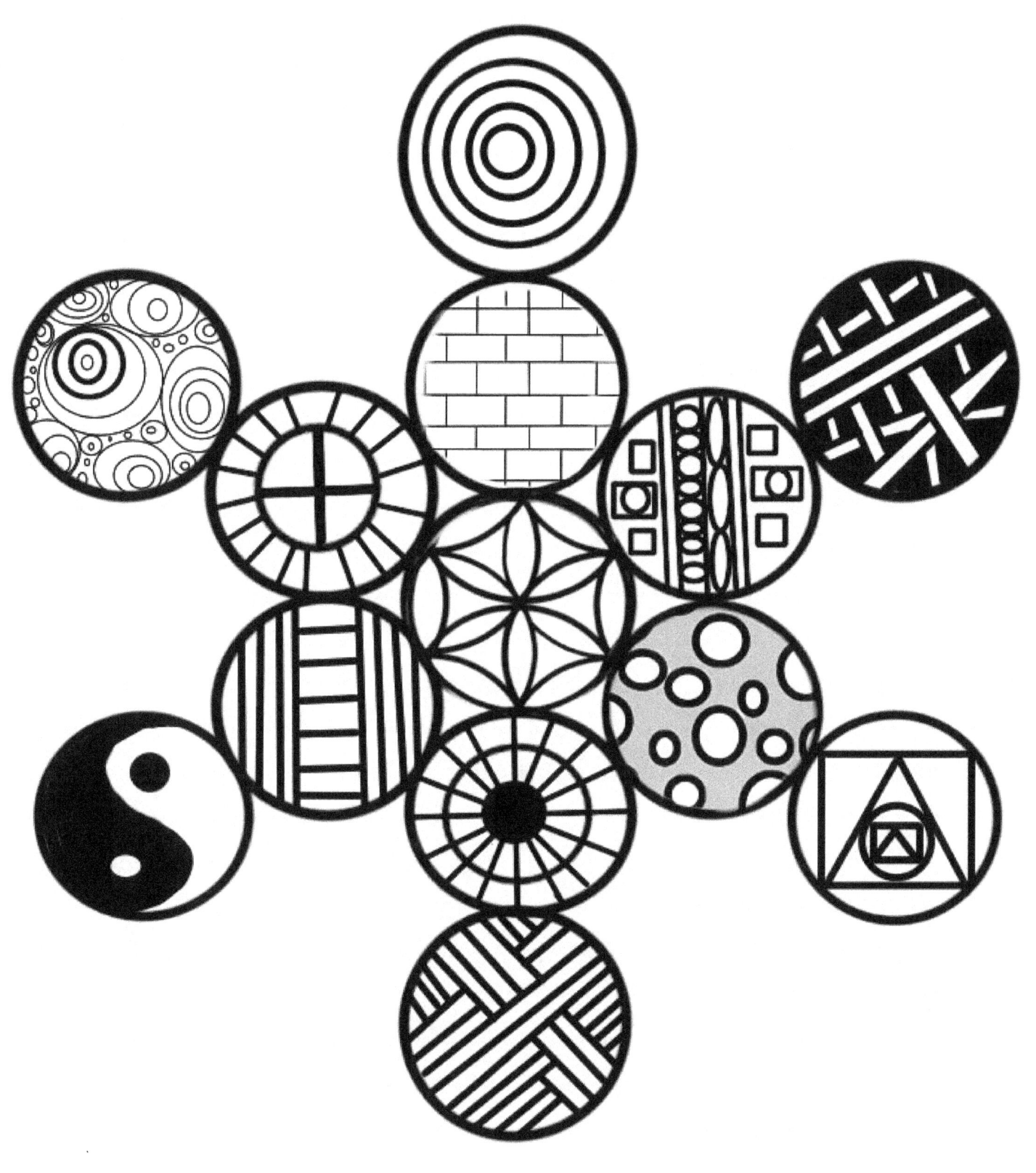

Fruit of Life

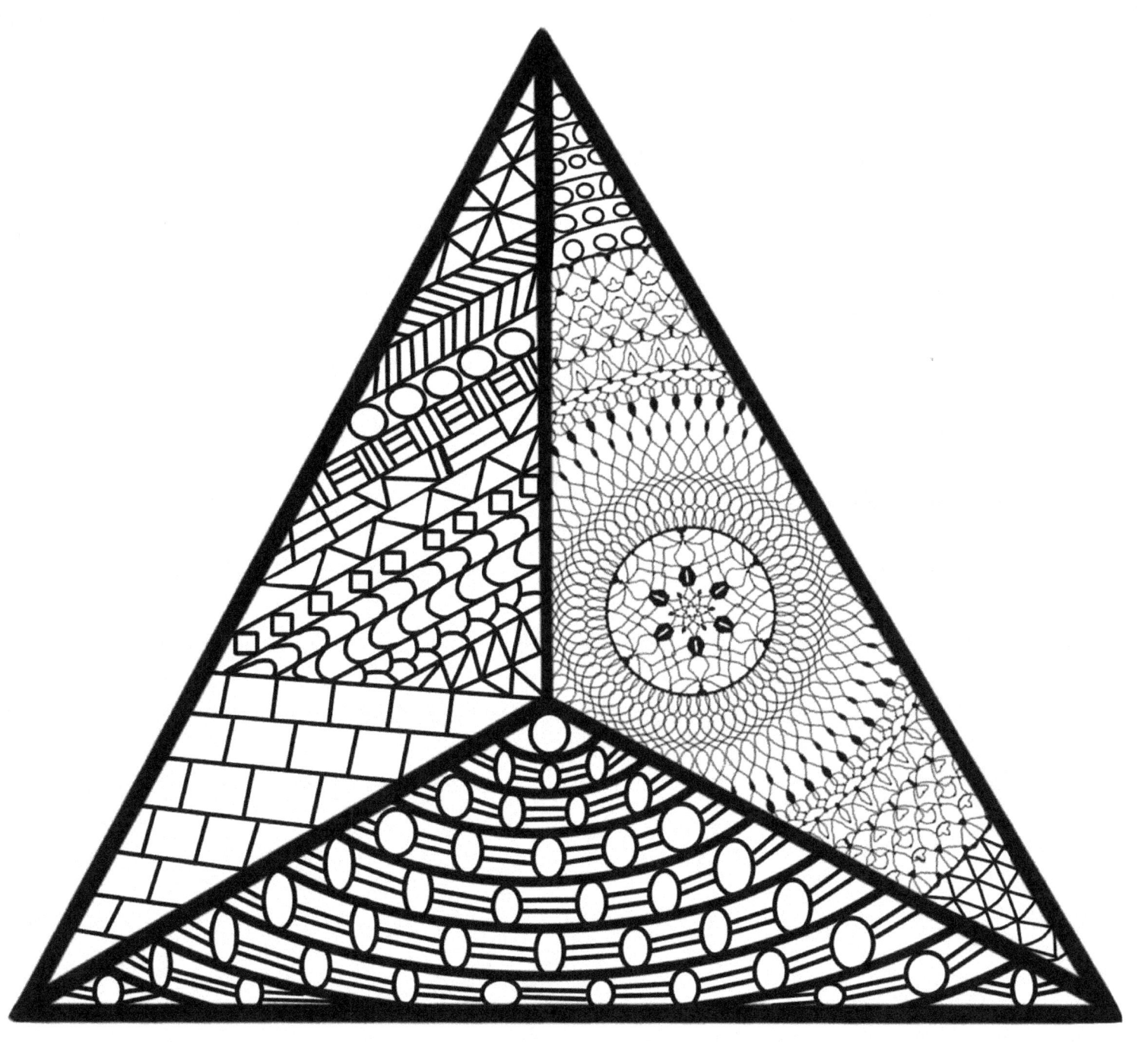

Tetrahedron

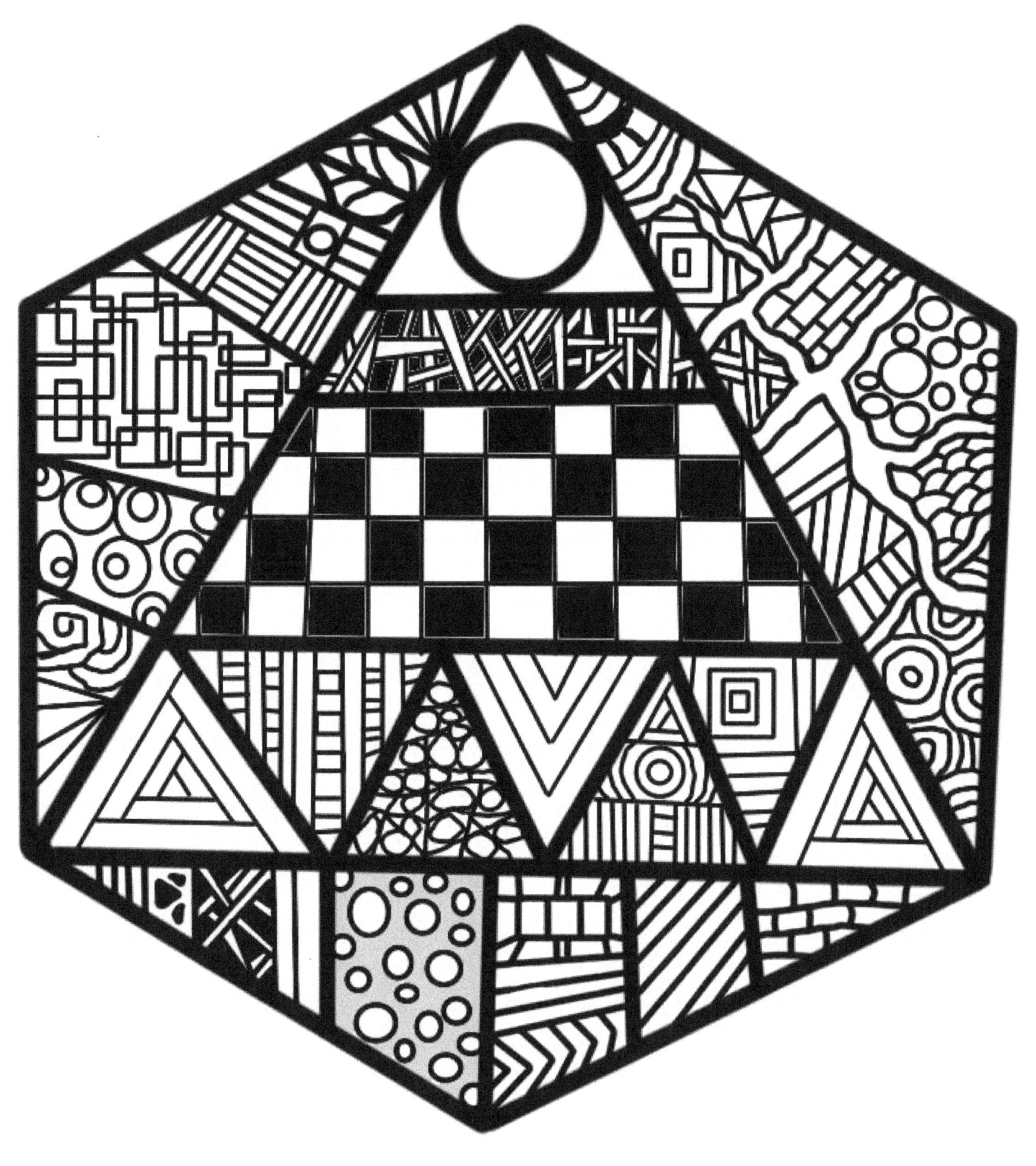

Octahedron

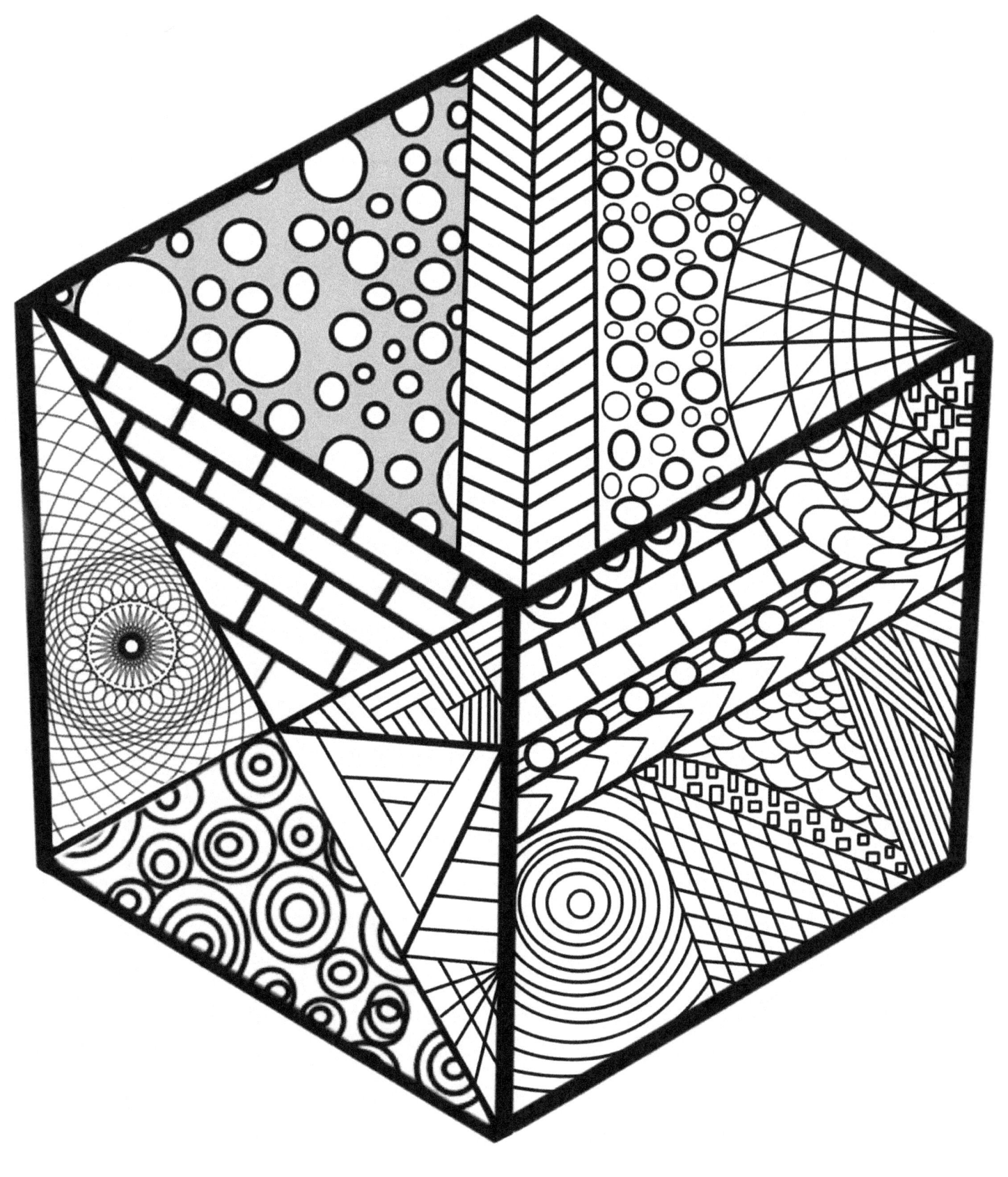

Hexahedron

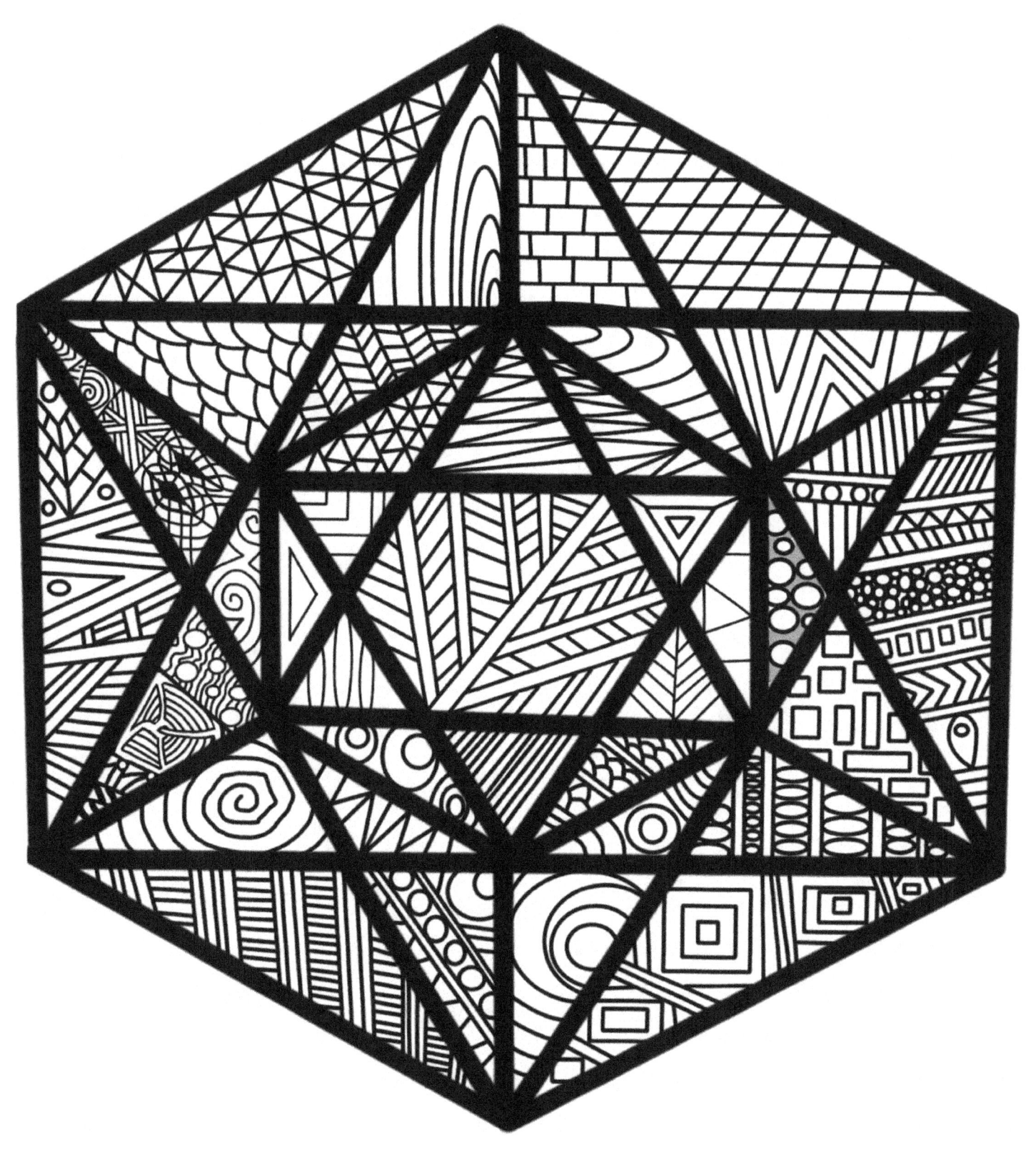

Icosahedron

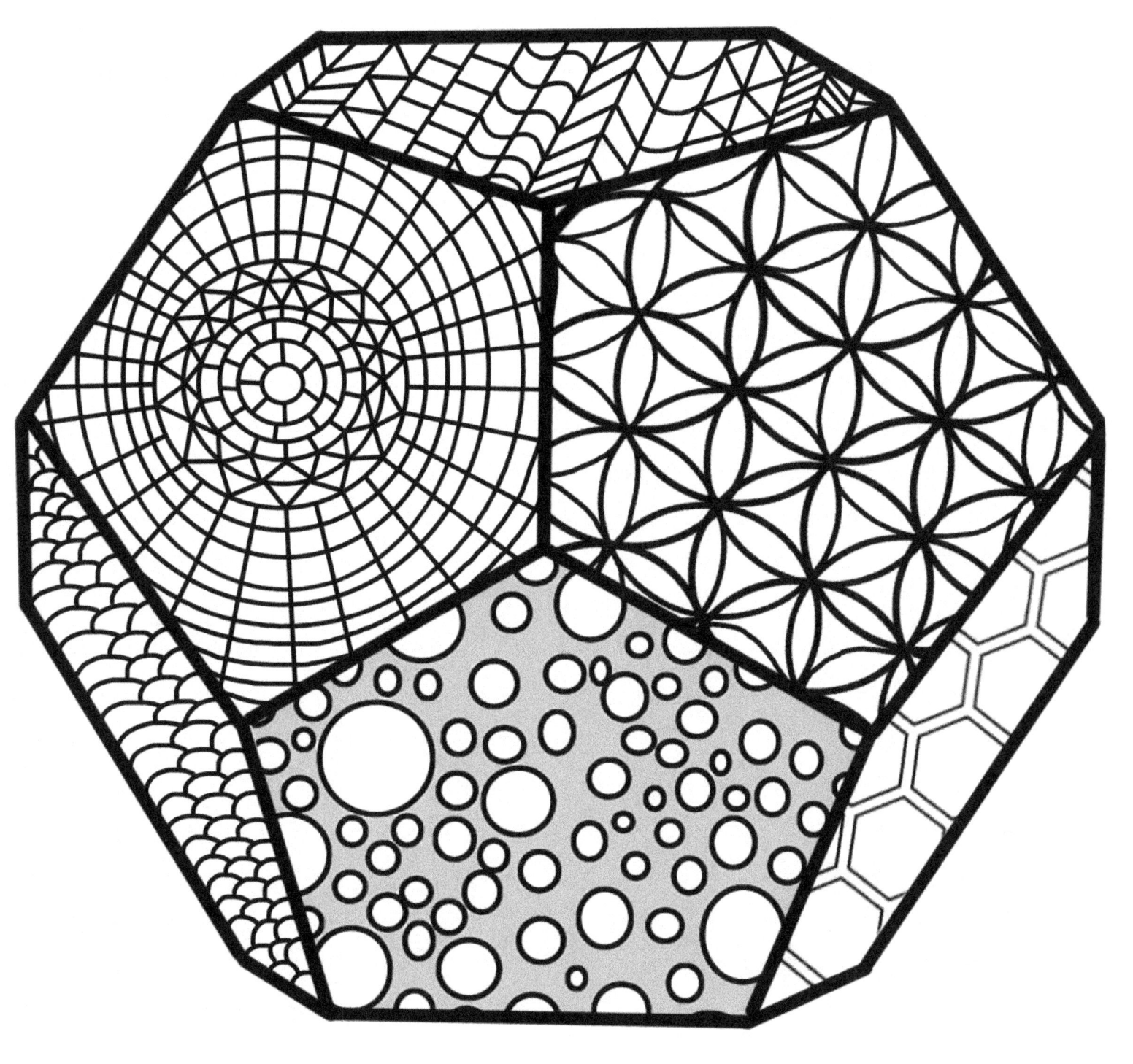

Dodecahedron

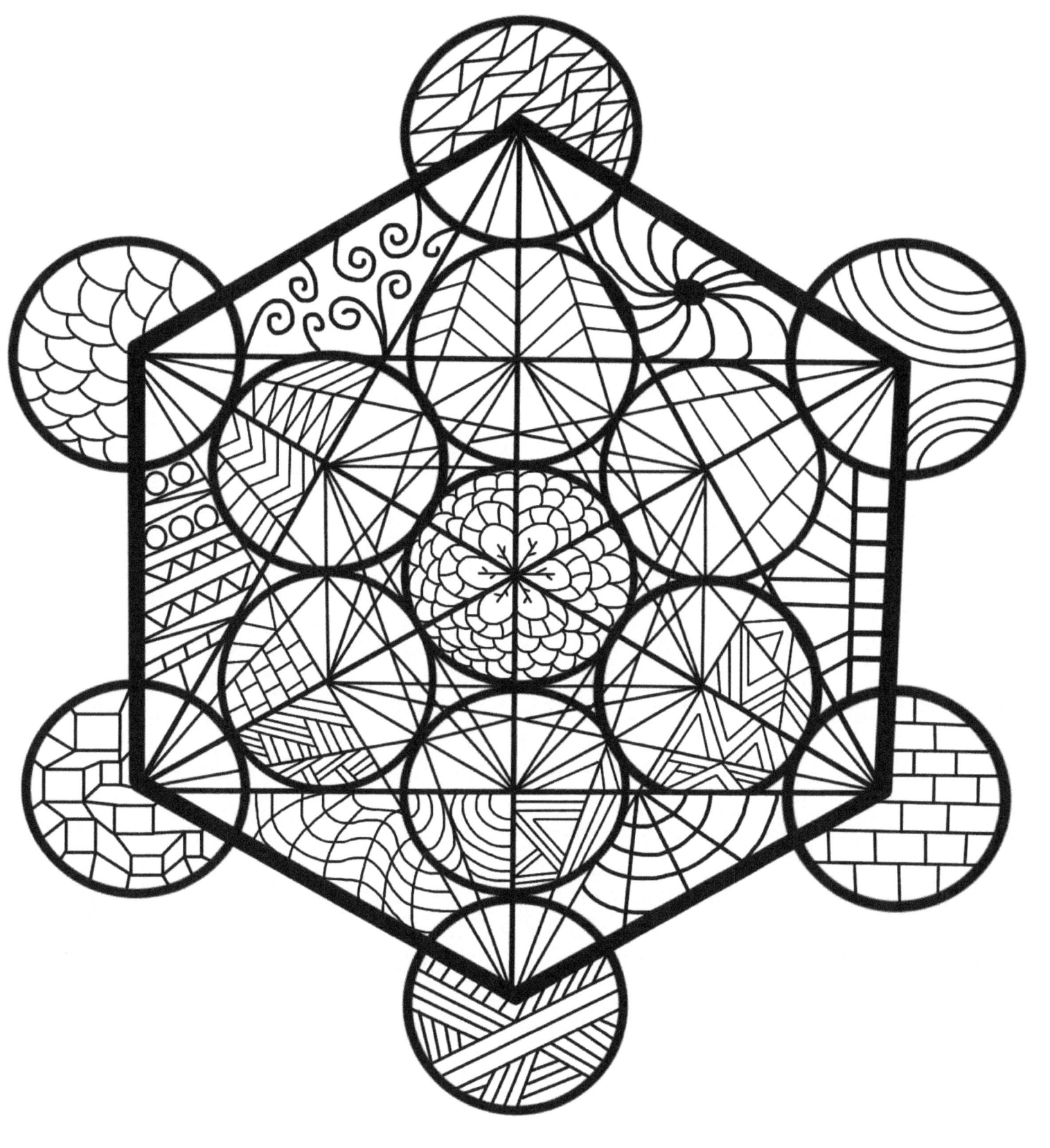

Metatron's Cube

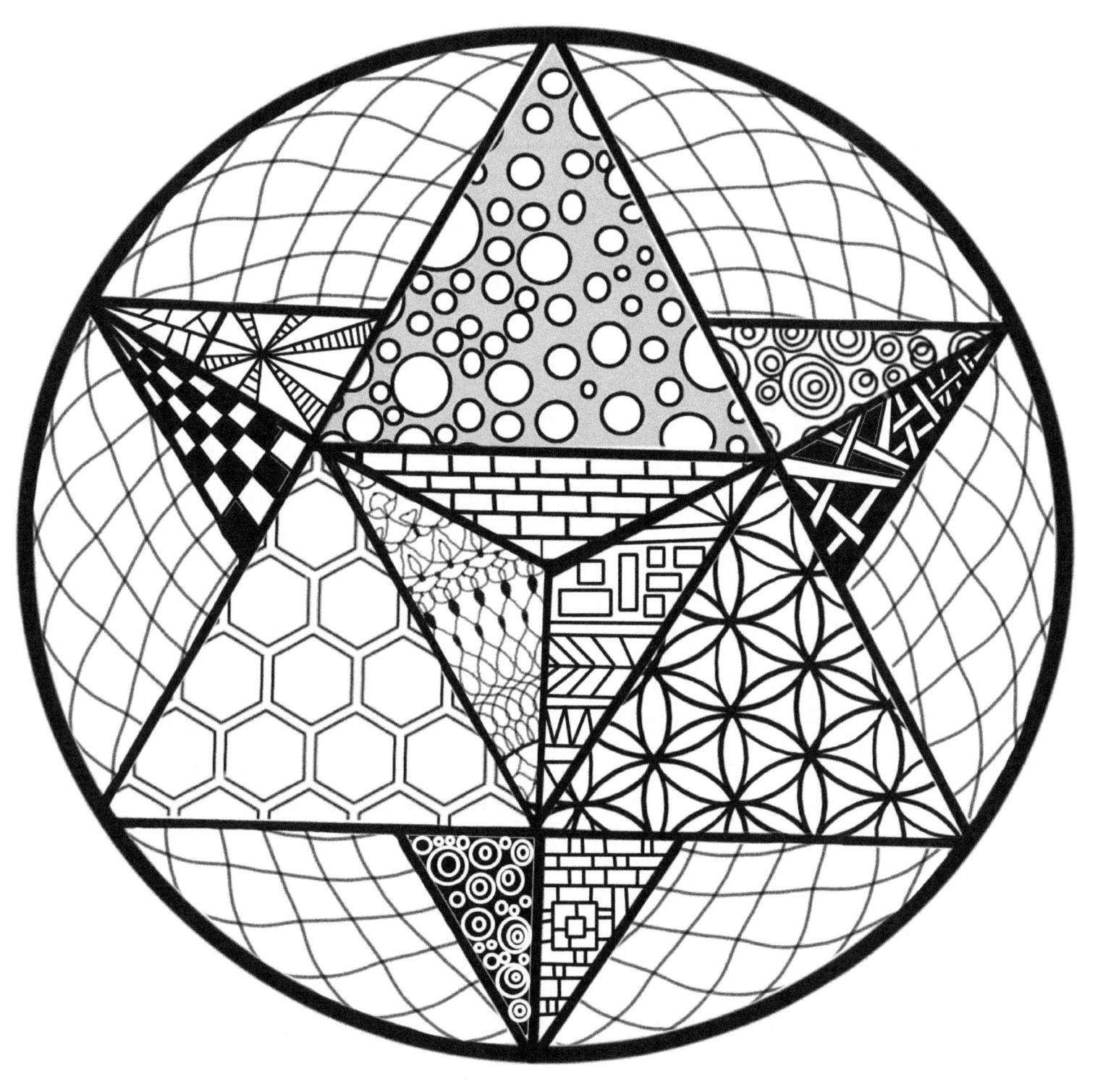

Merkaba

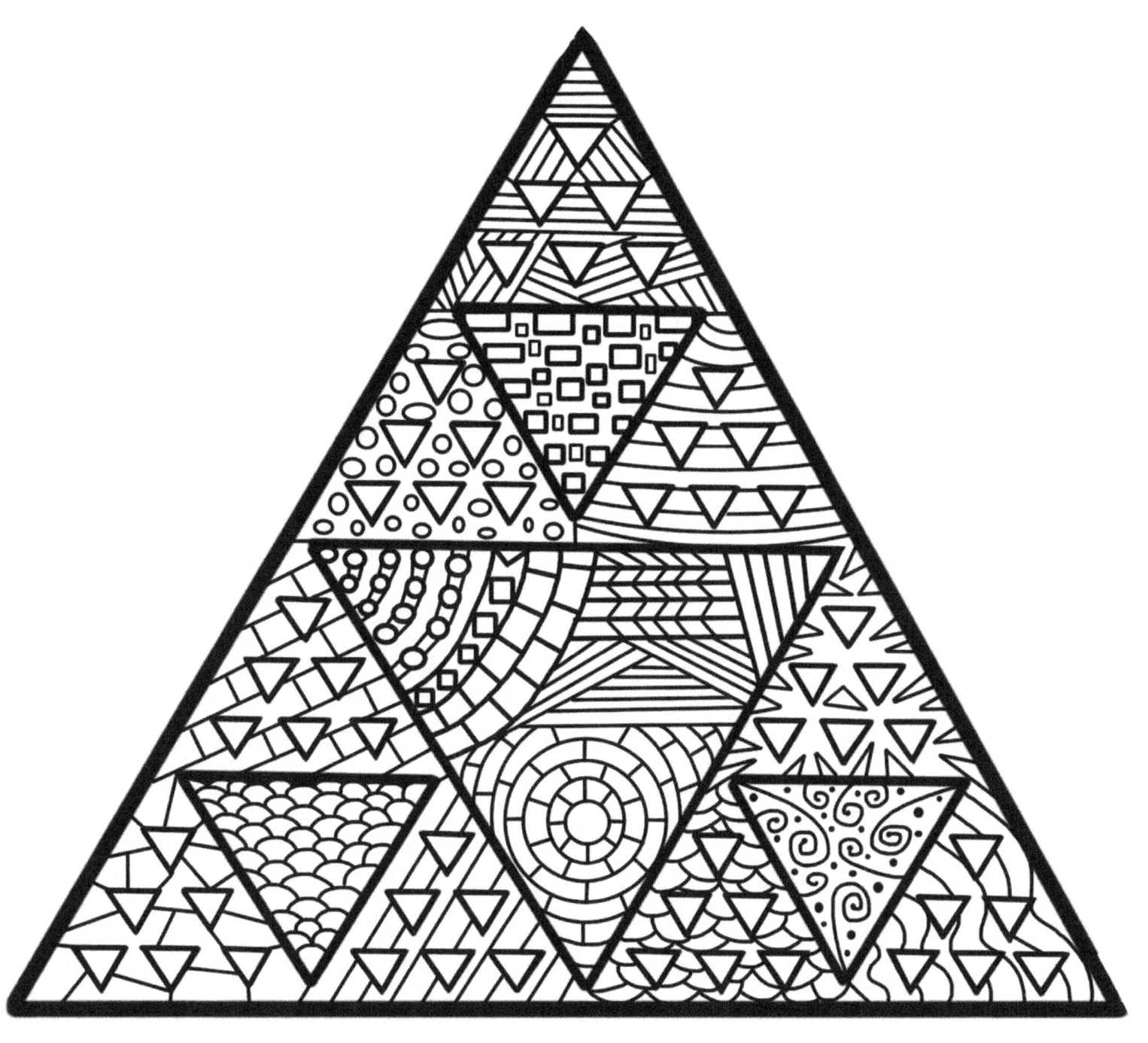

Fractal

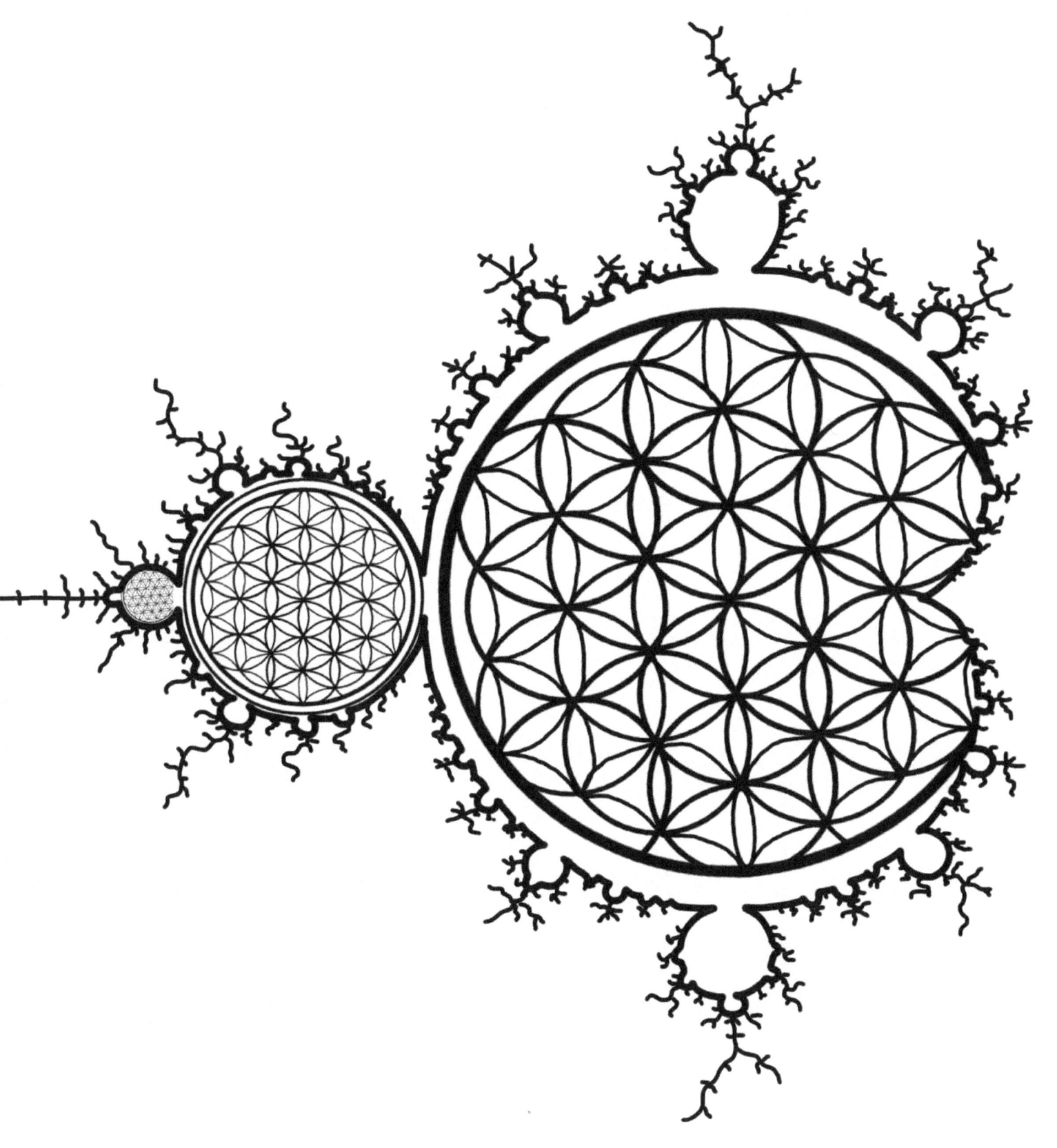

Mandelbrot

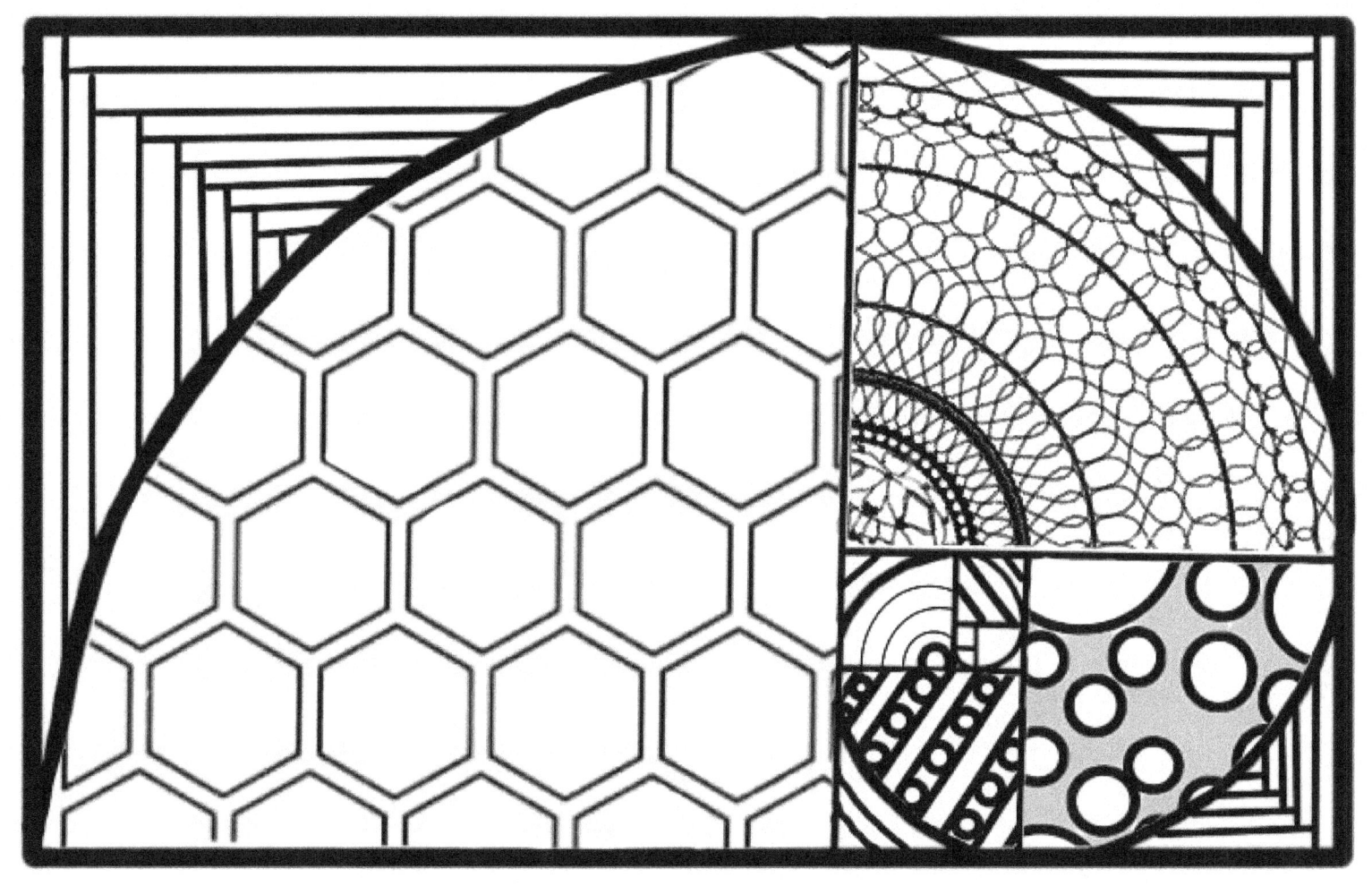

Fibonacci

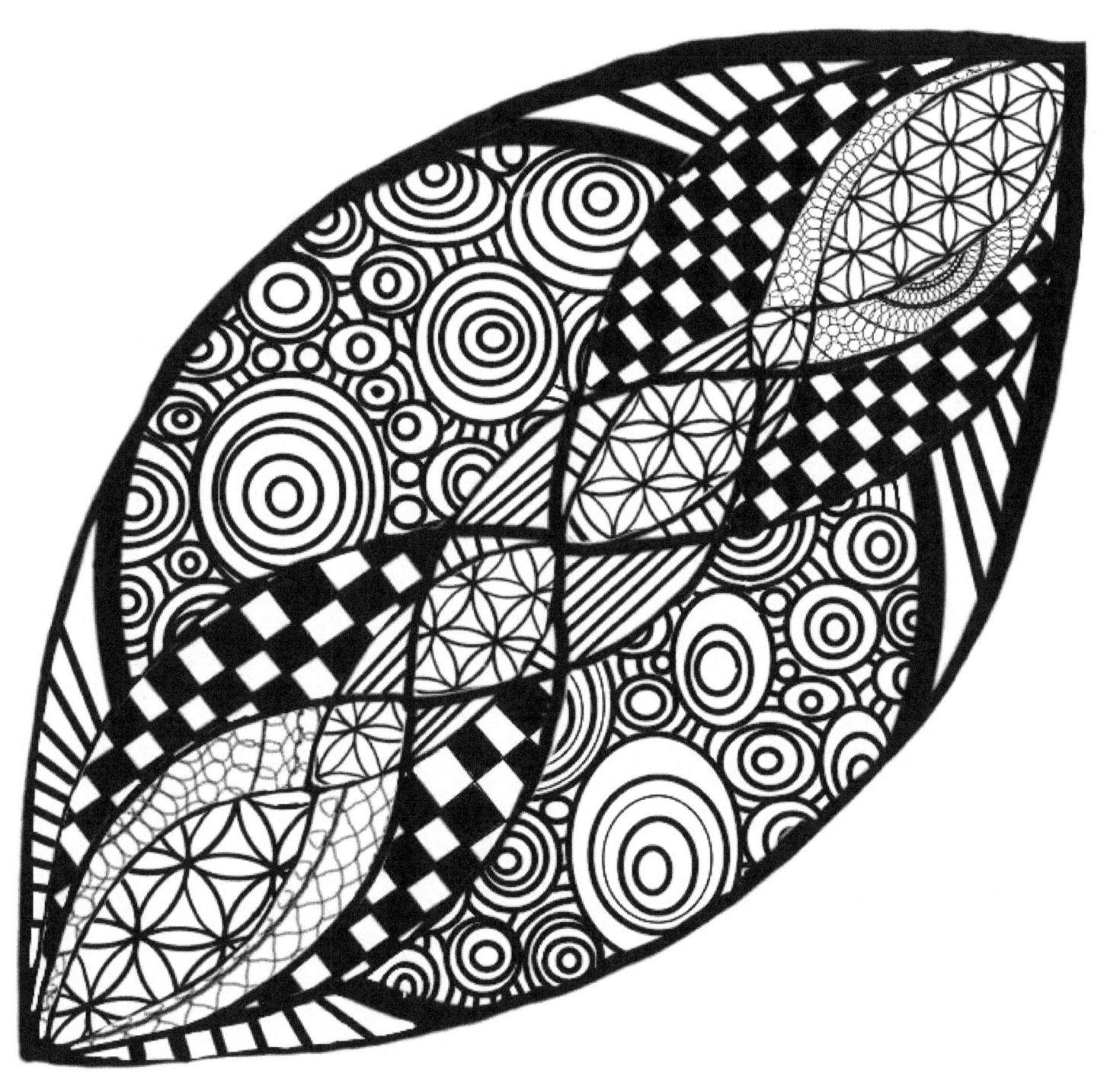

Harmonics

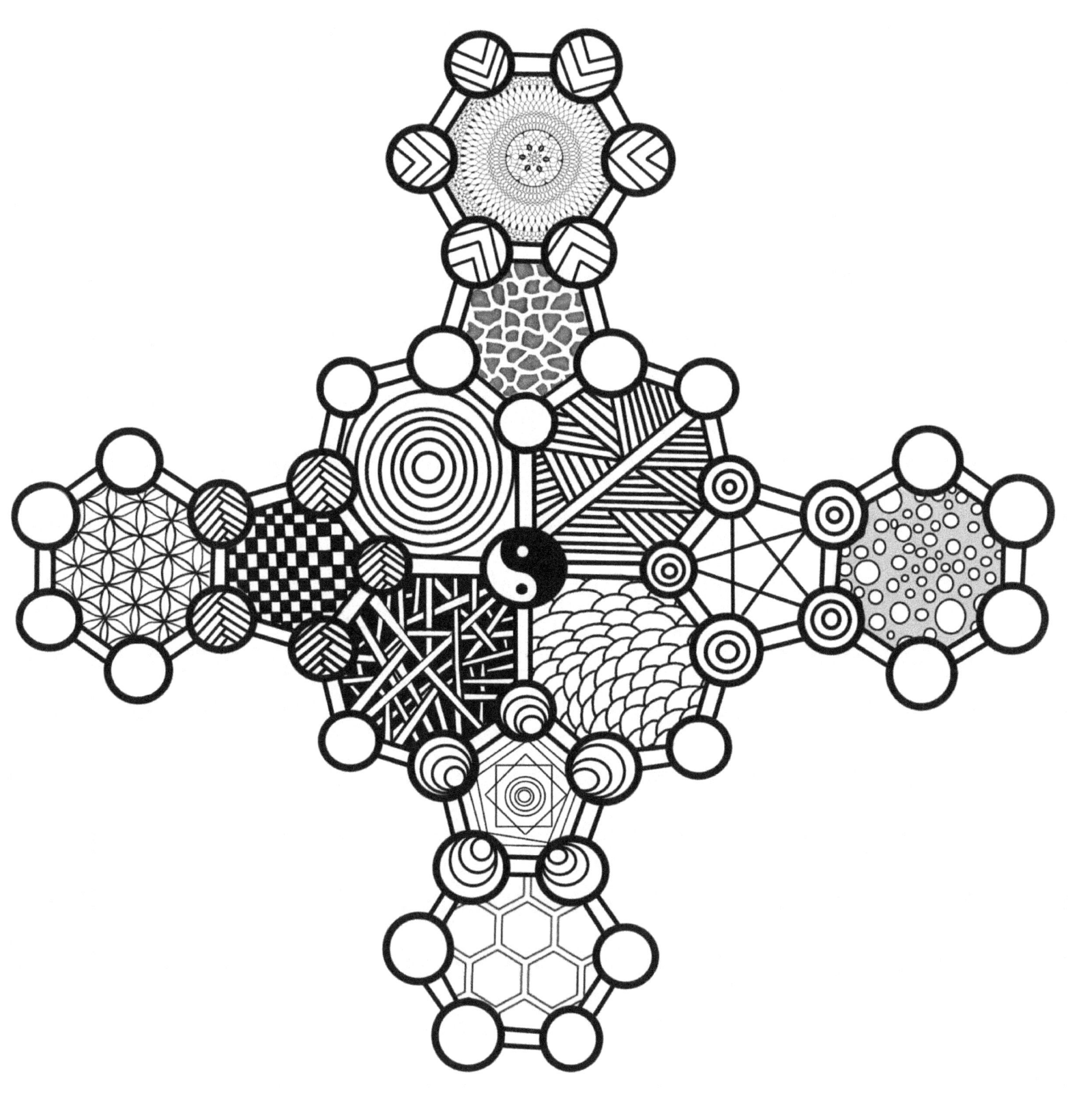

Molecule

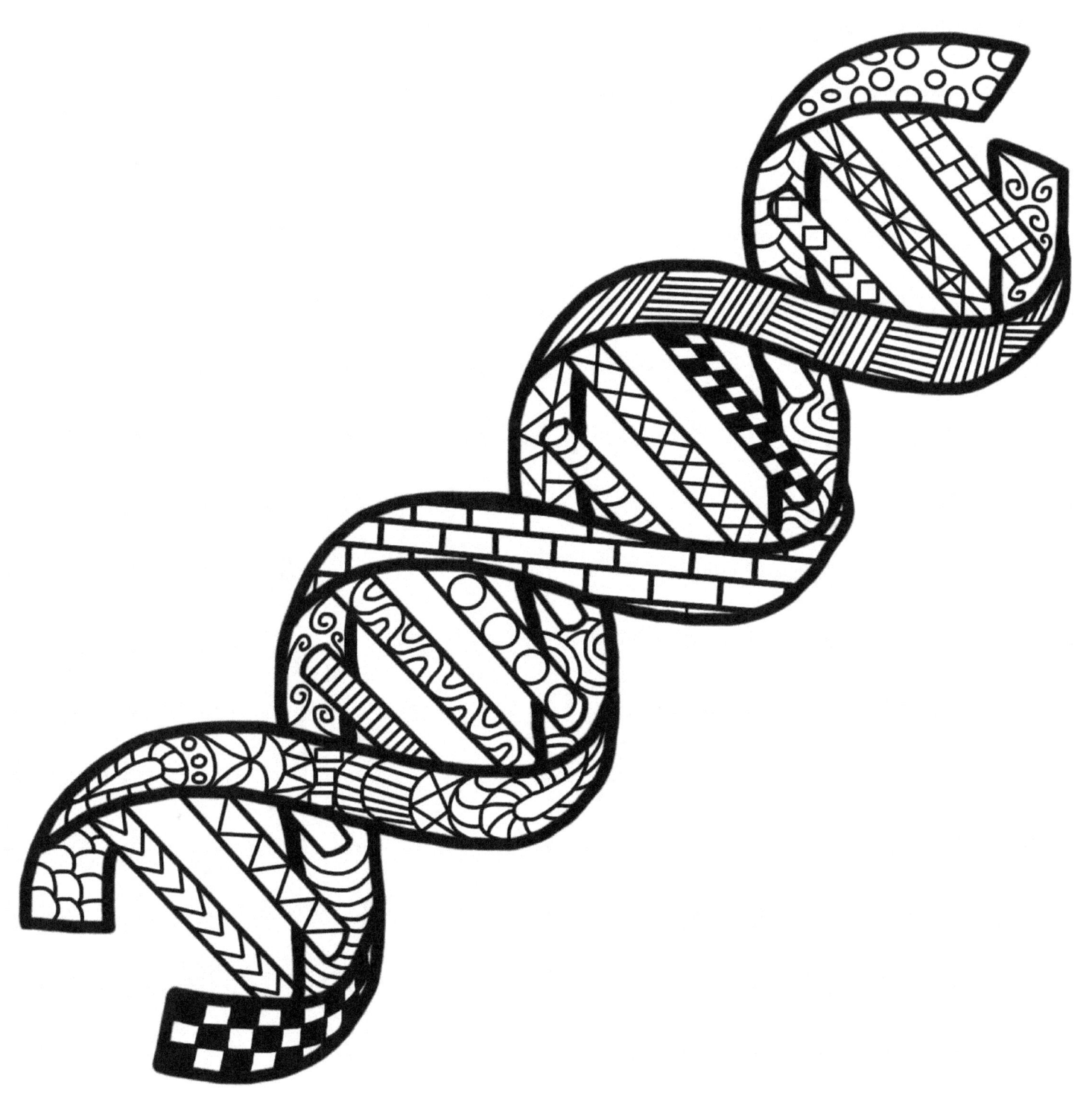

DNA

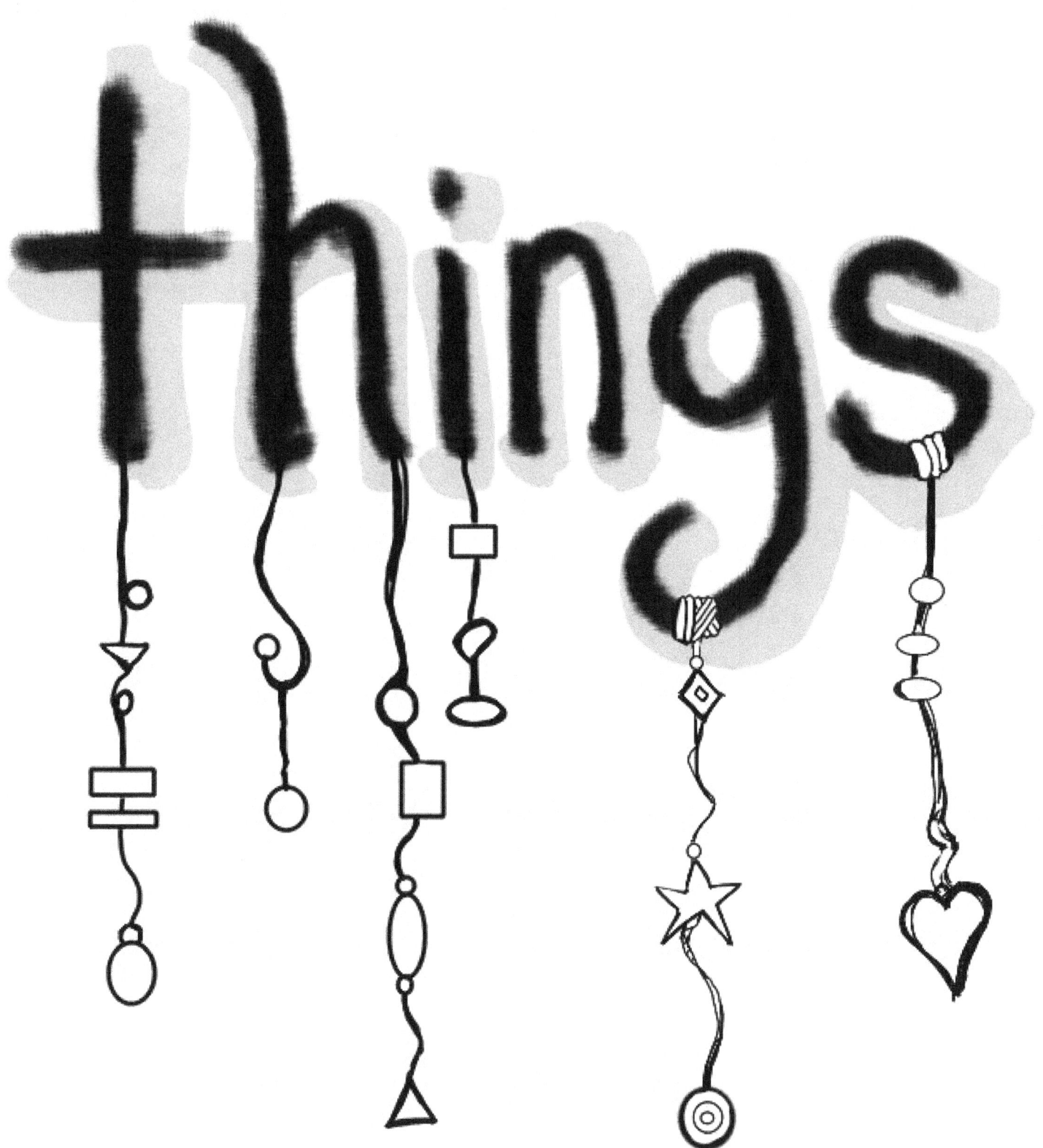

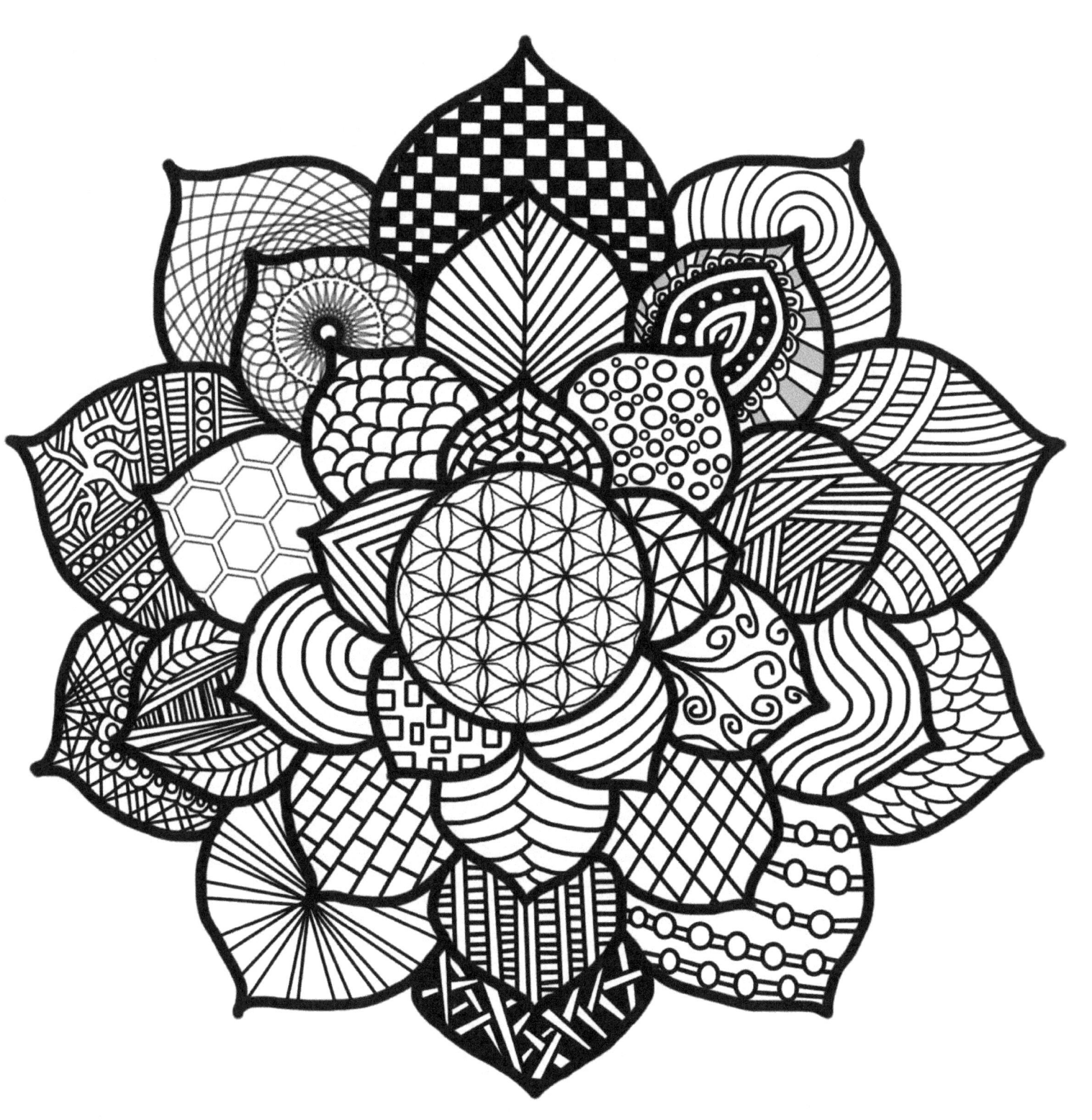

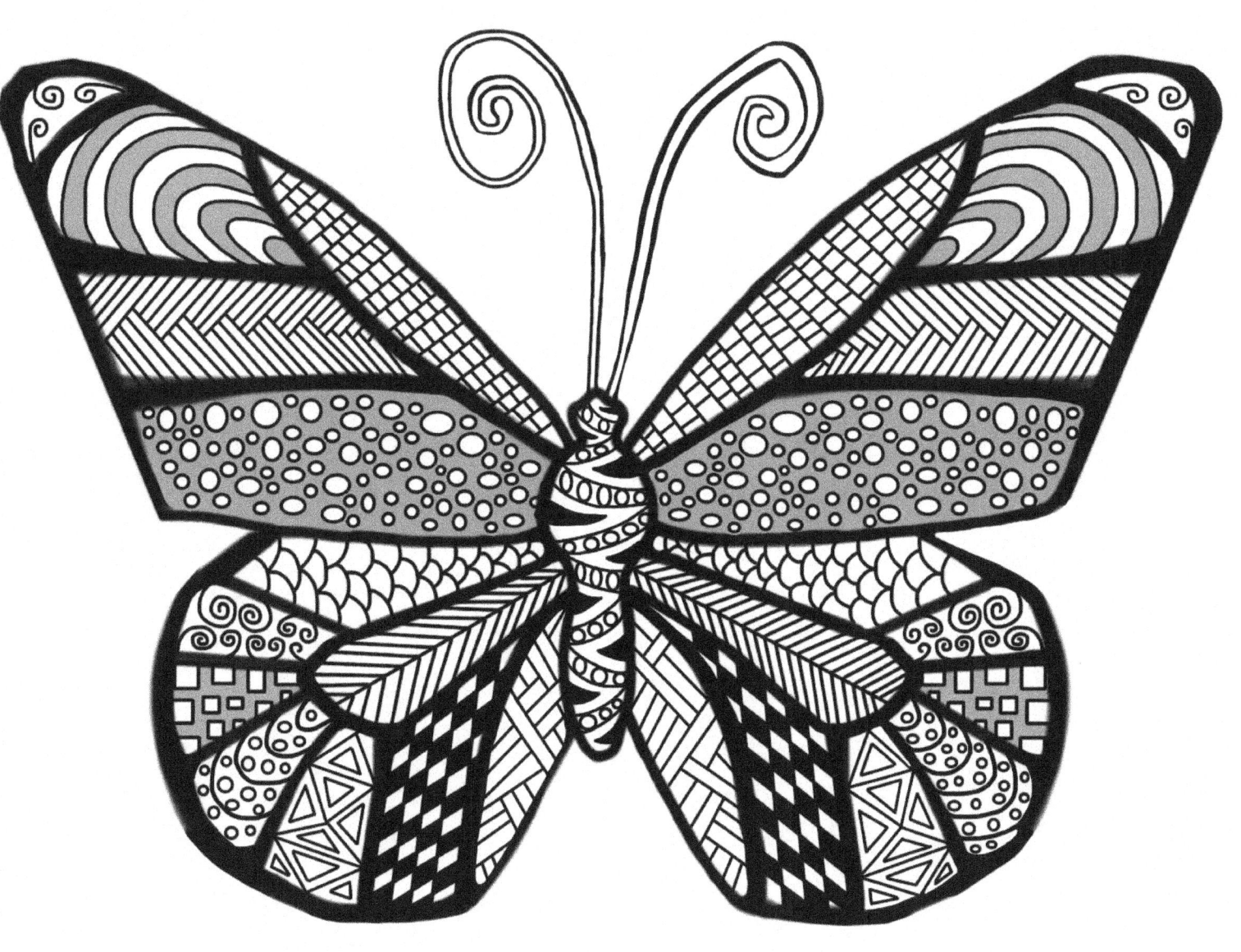

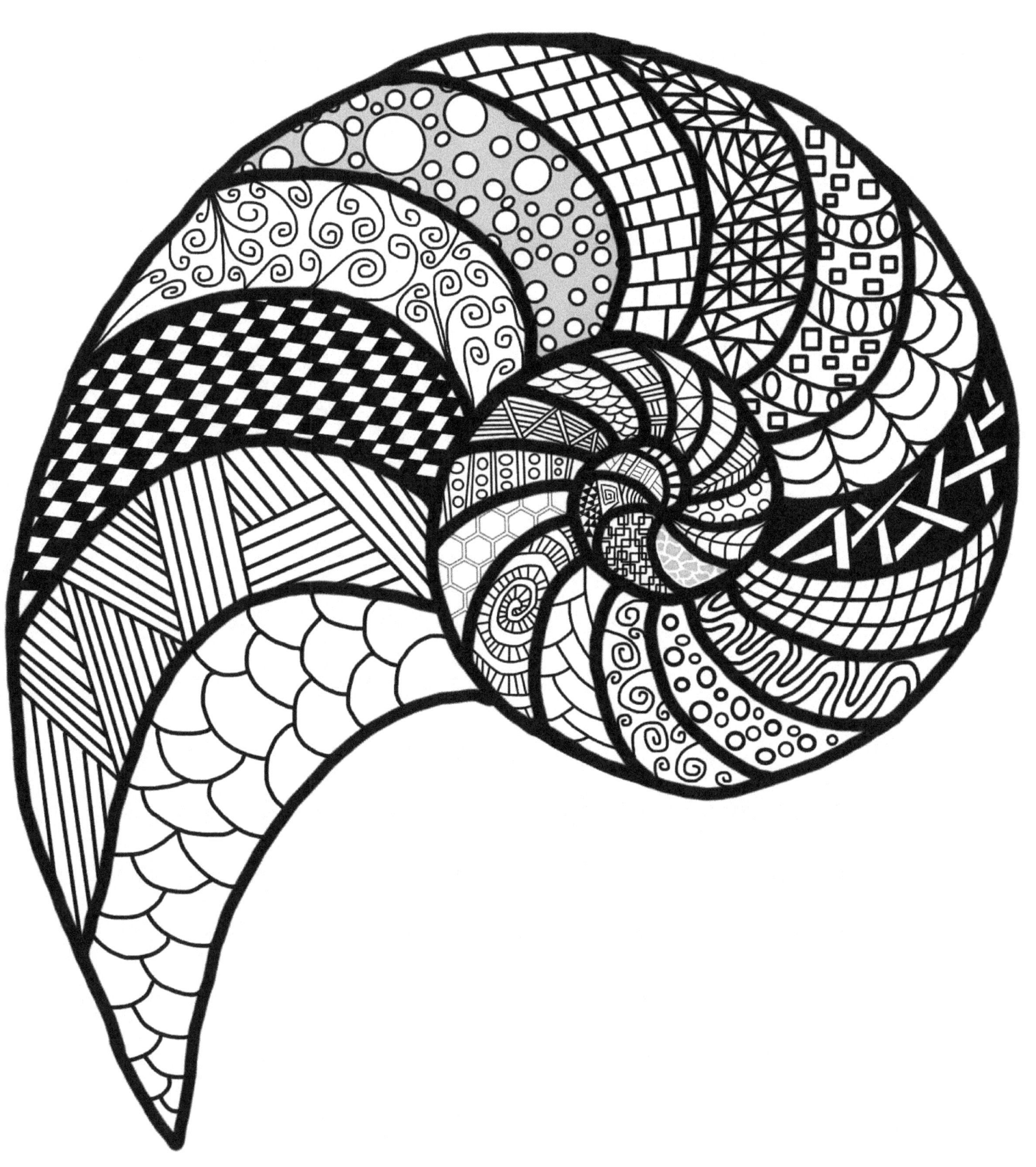

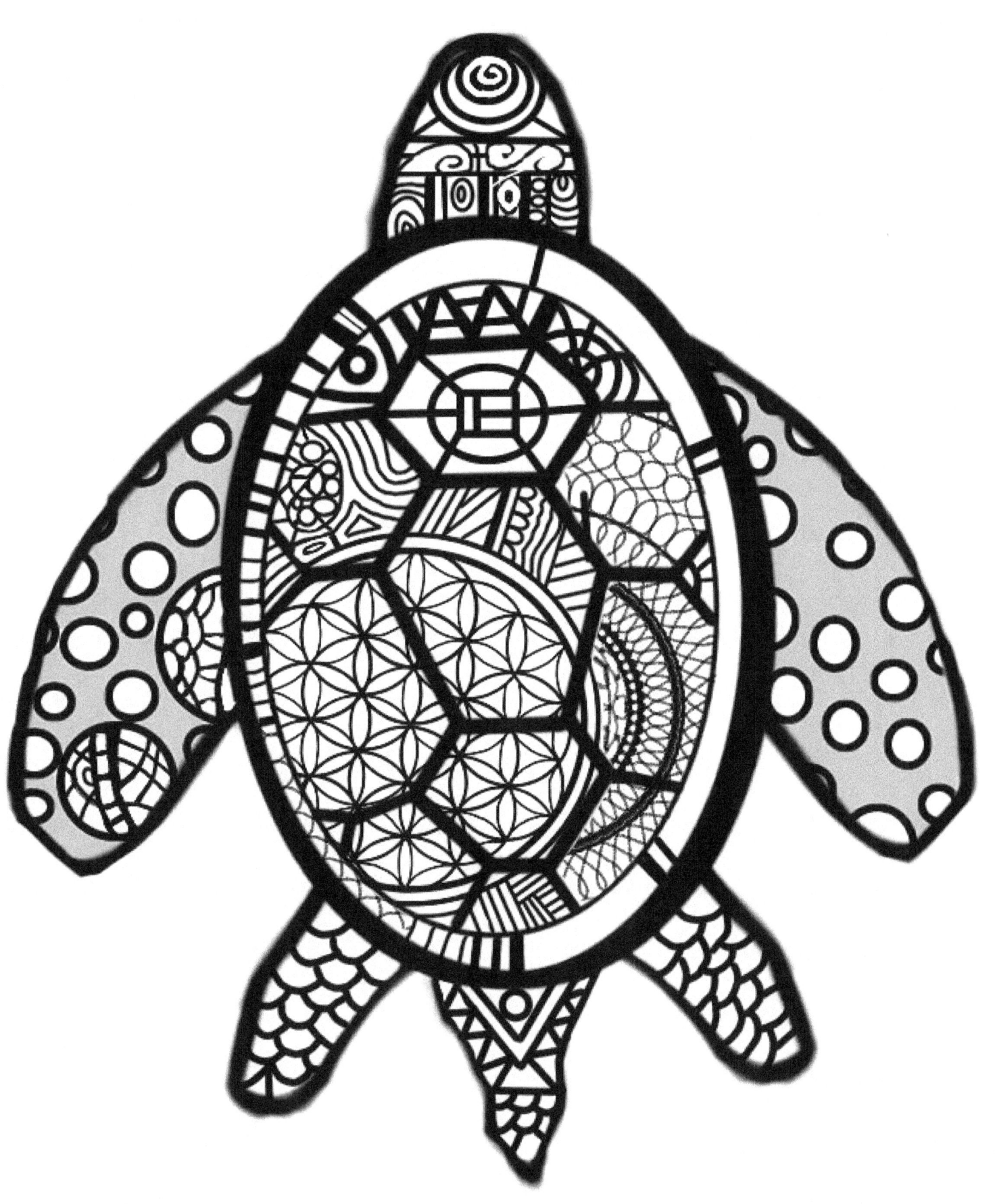

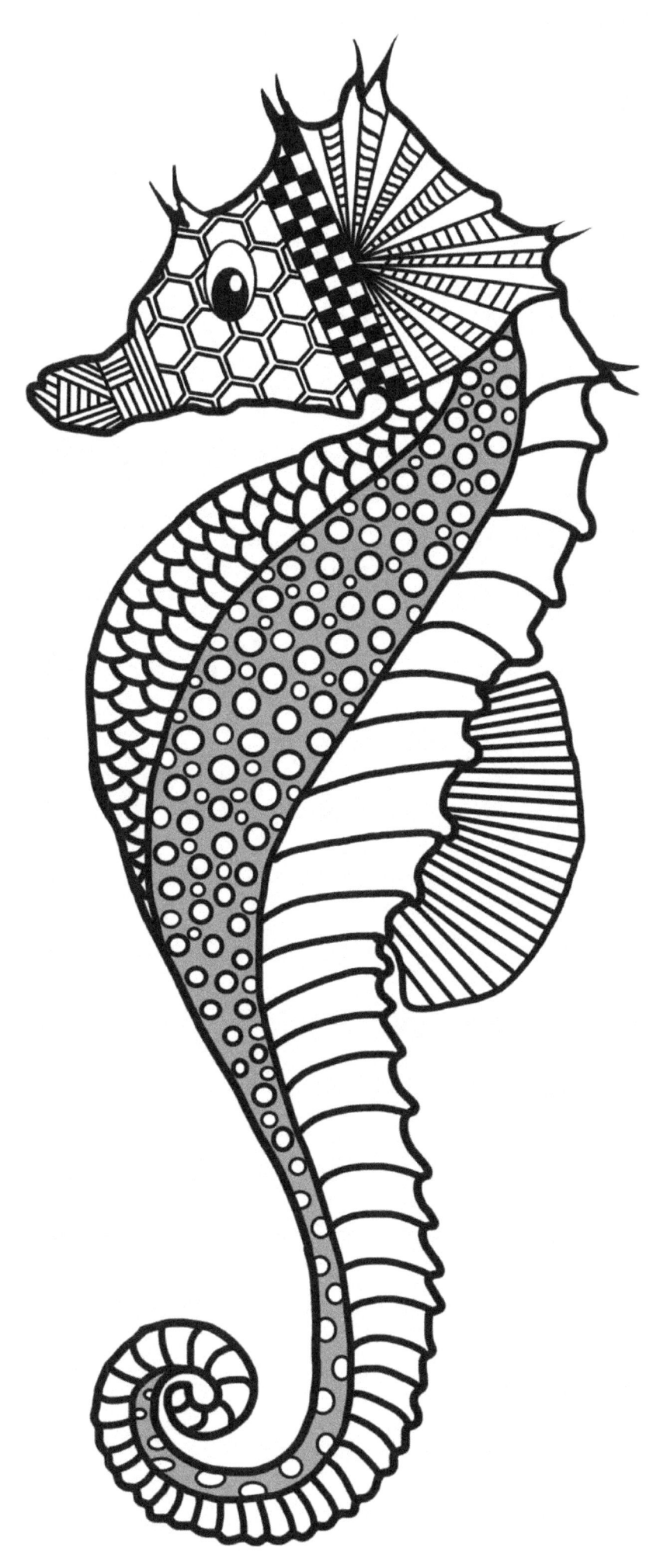

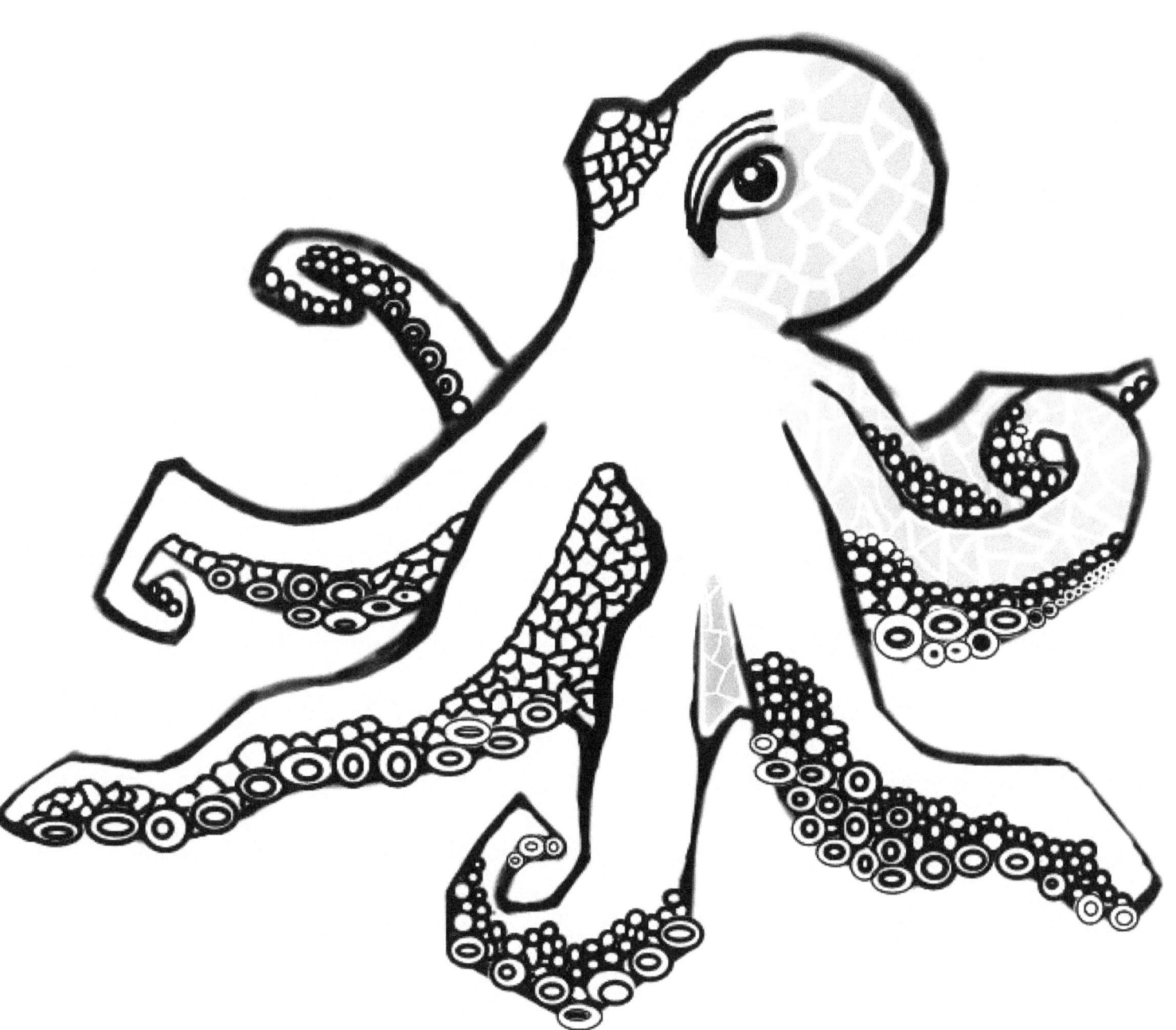

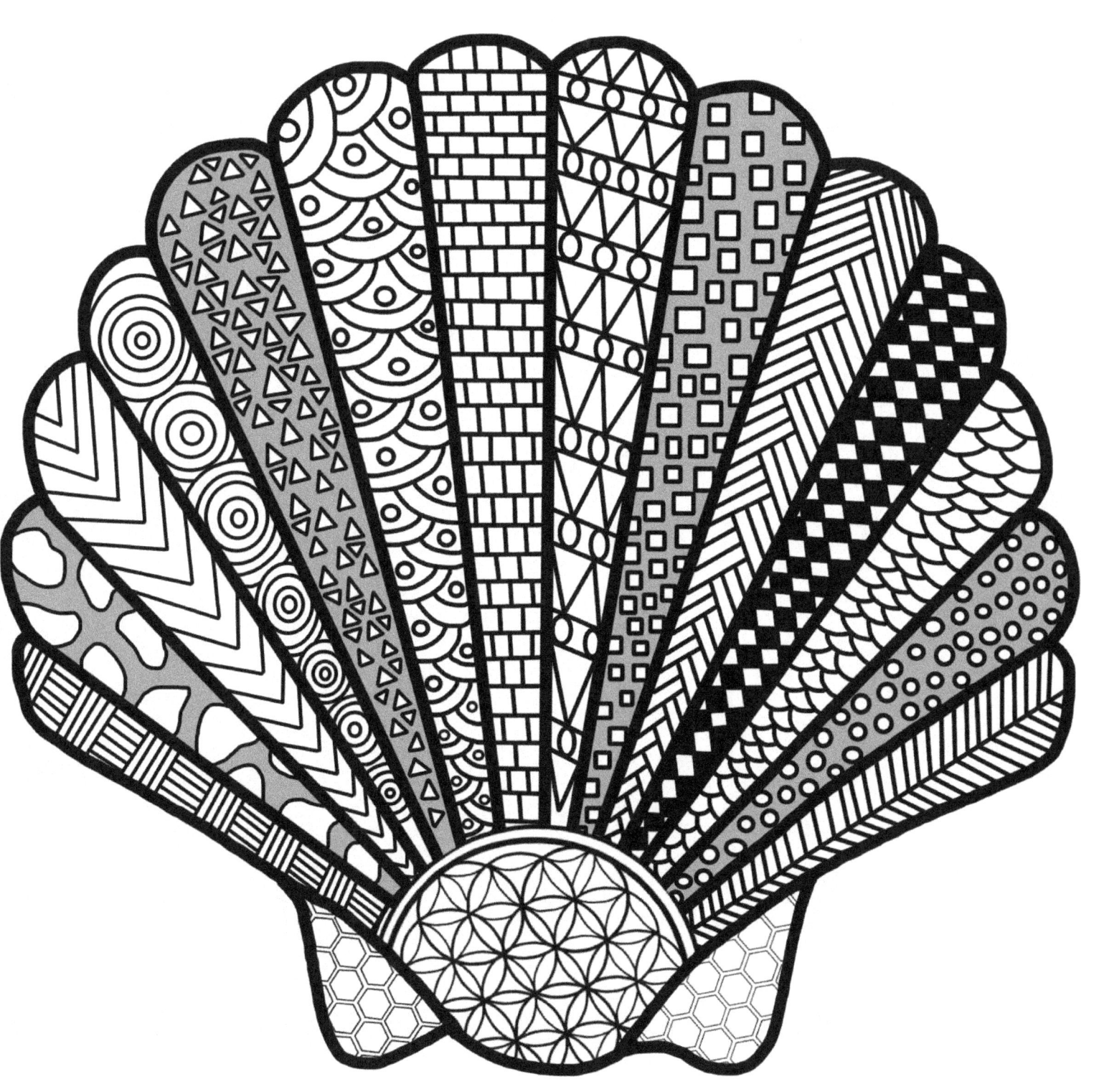

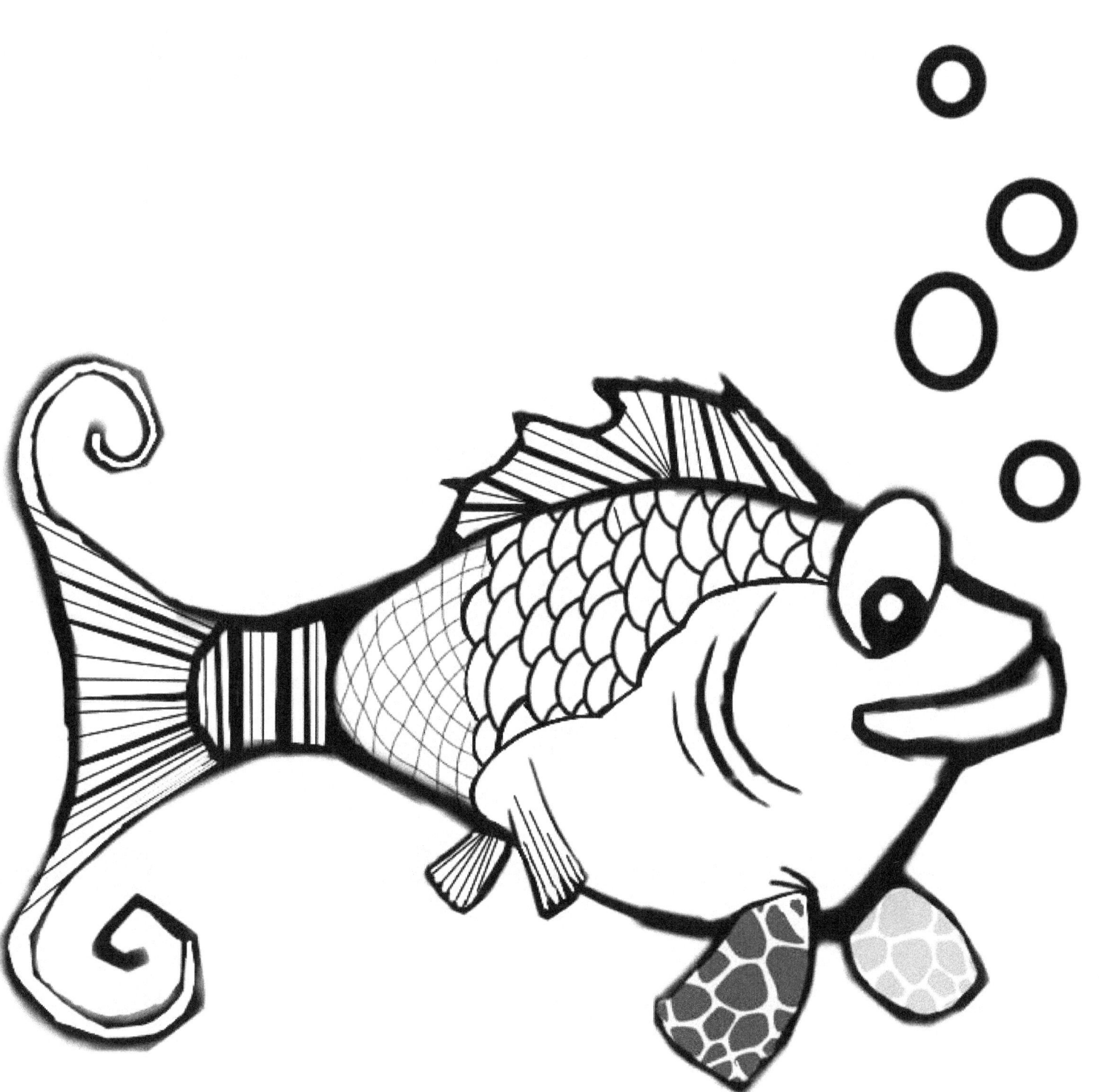

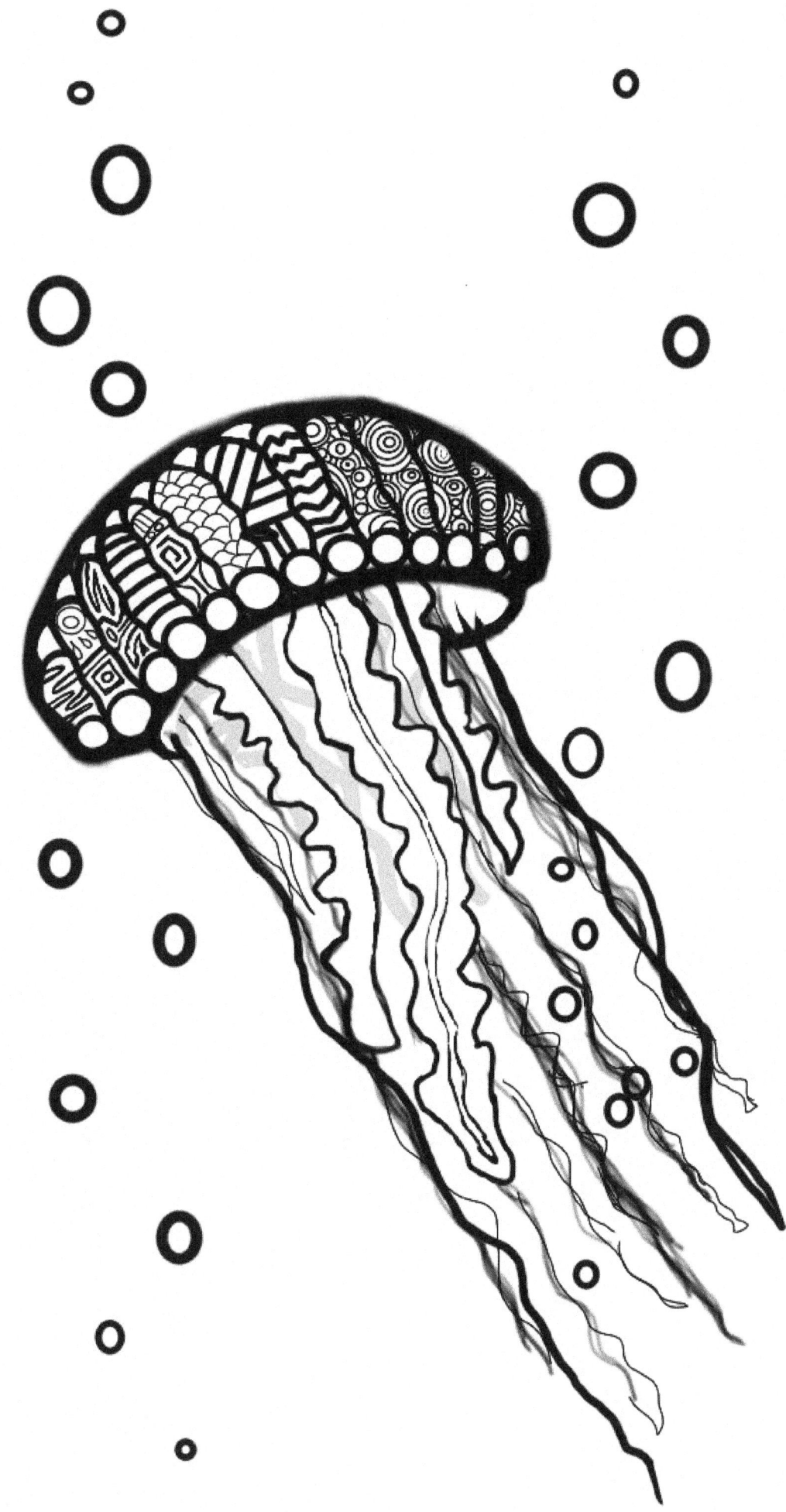

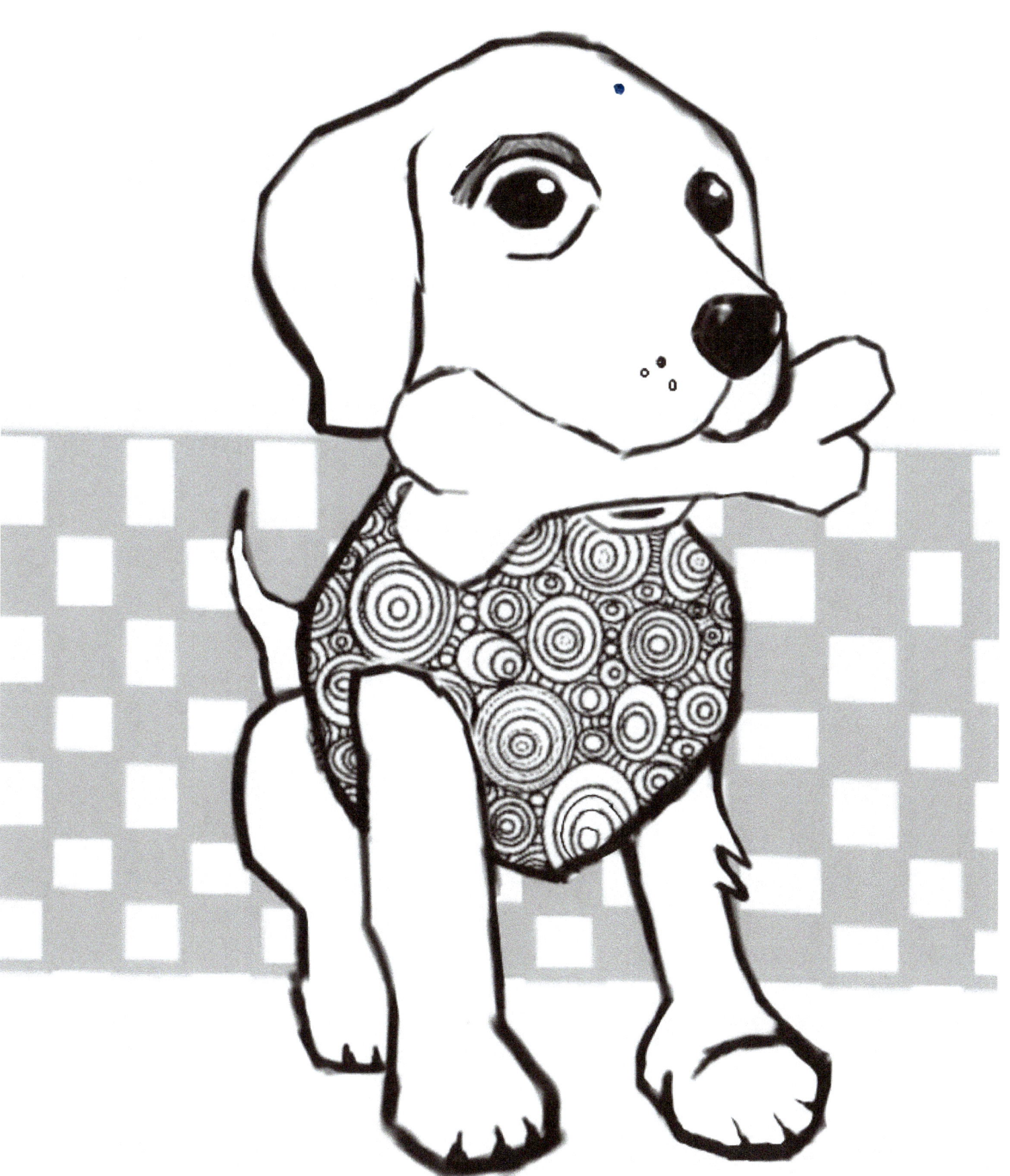

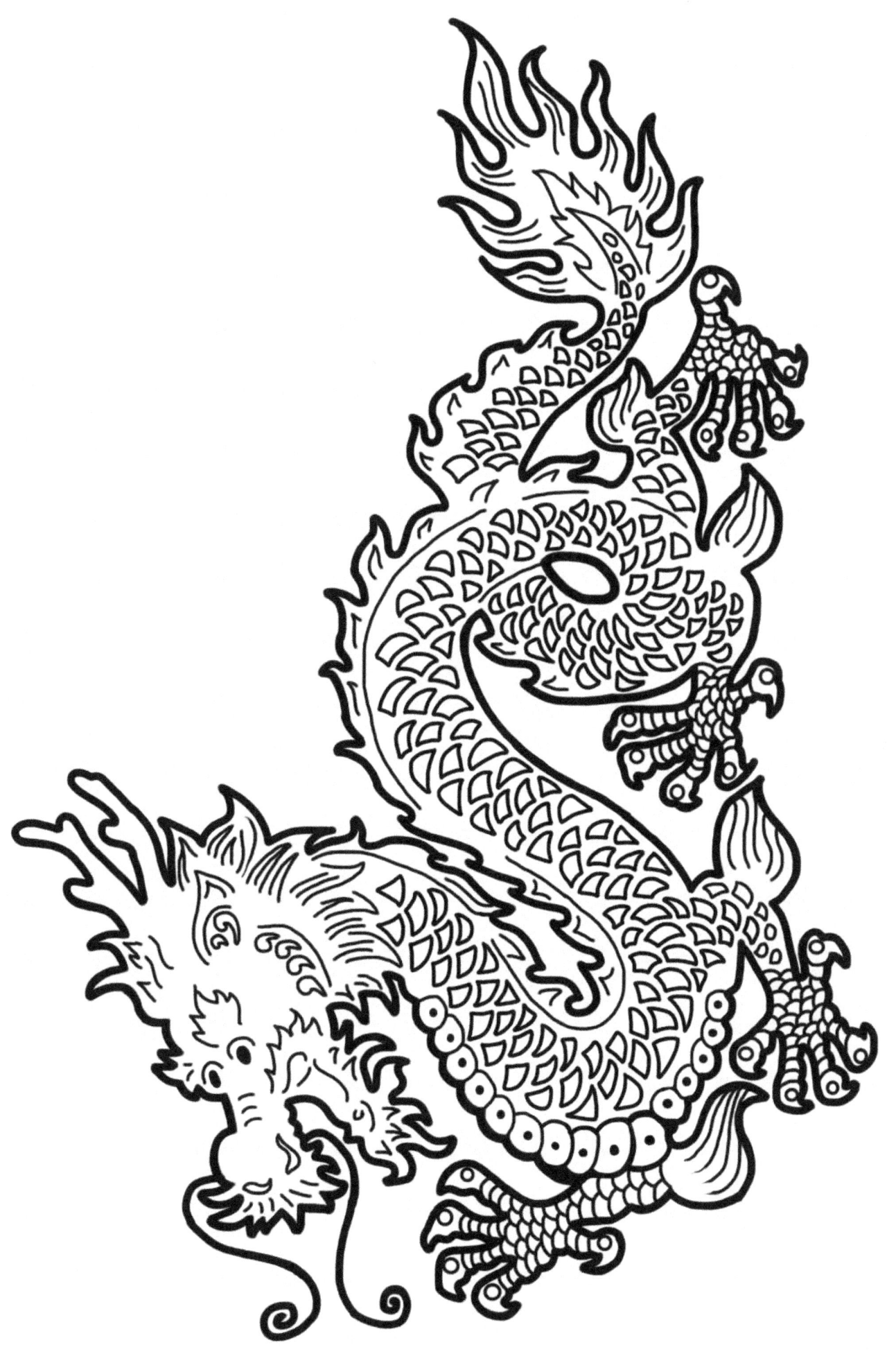

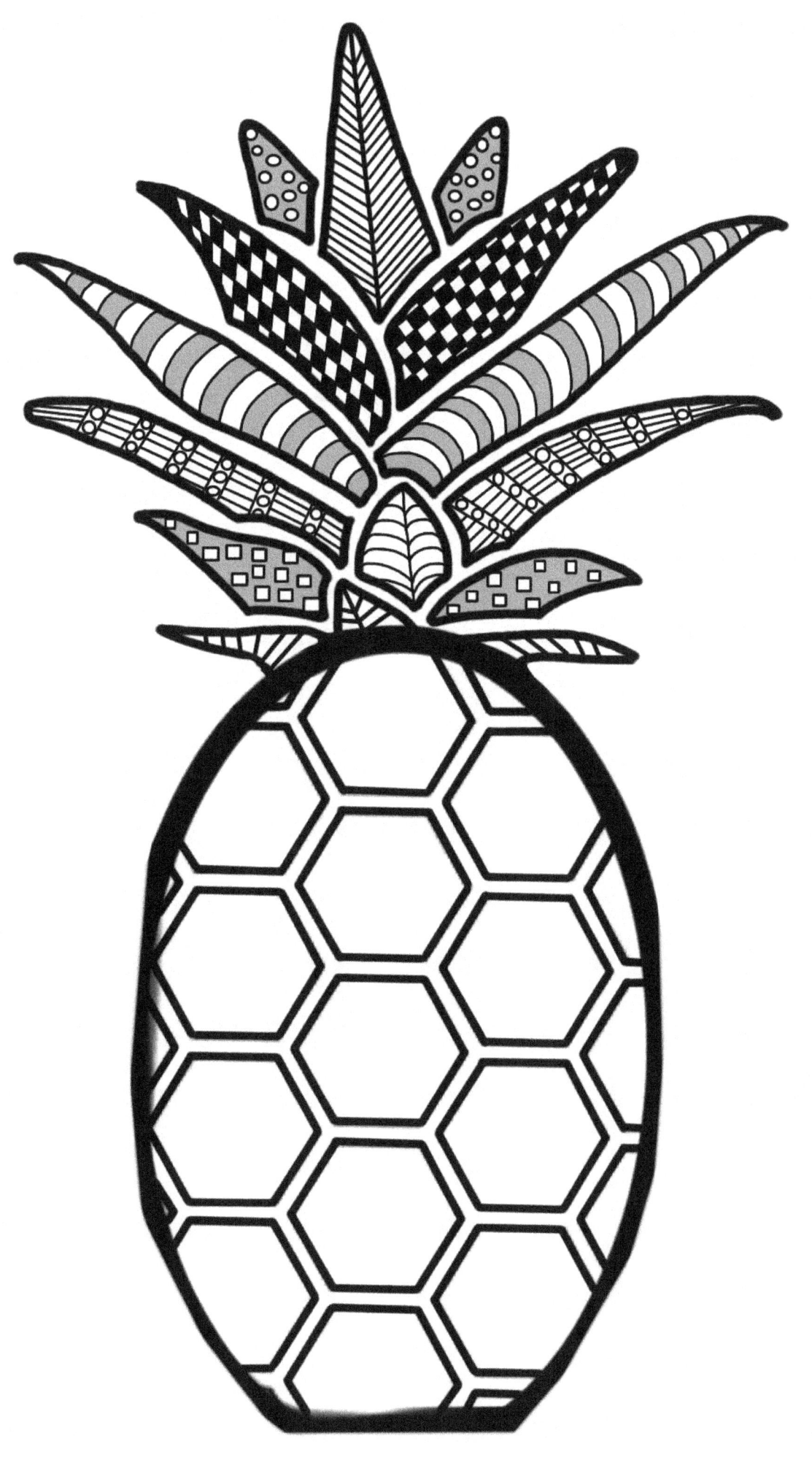

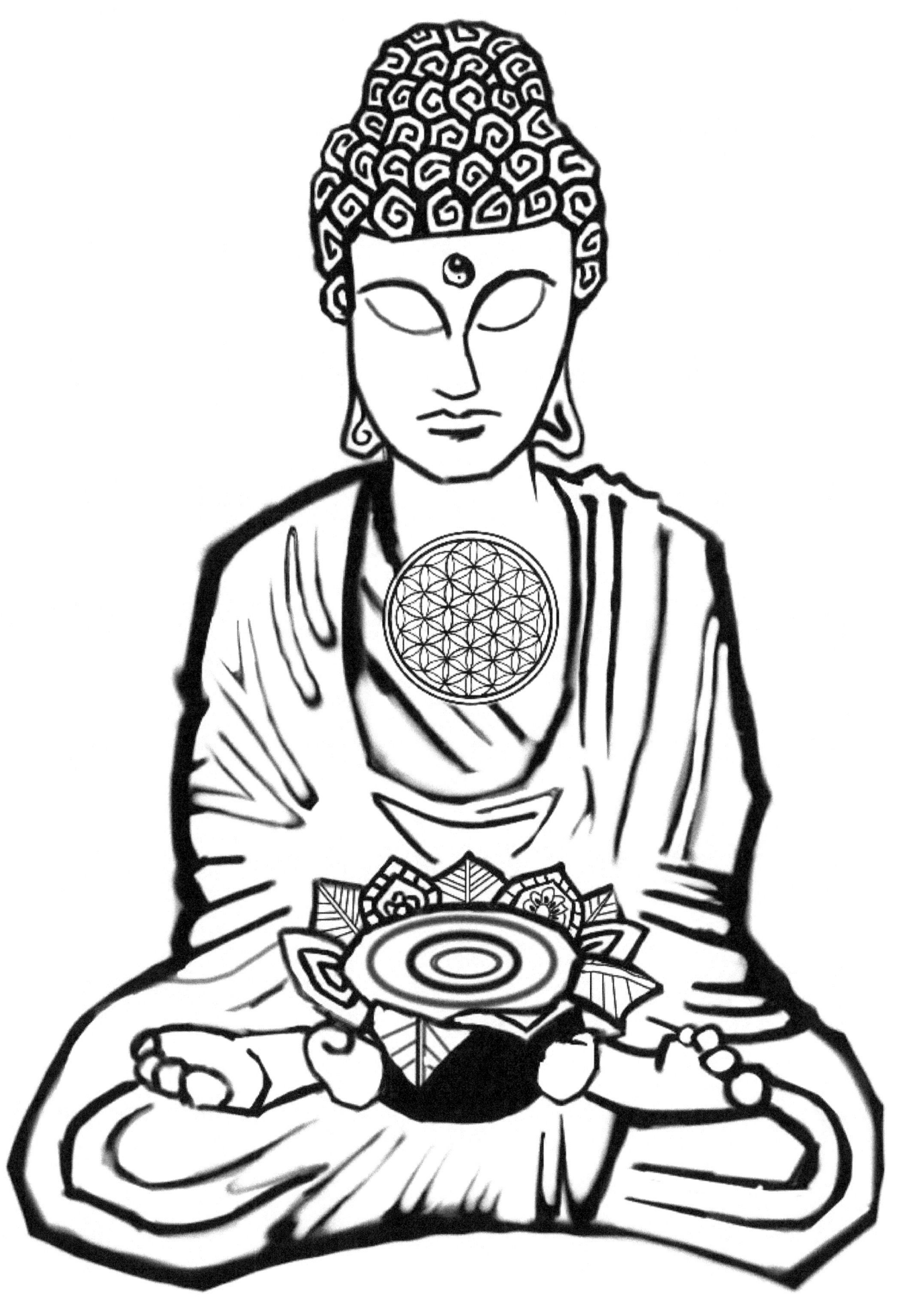